IAN MICHAEL WOOD

# History of the Totenkopf's Panther-Abteilung

★ ★ ★

peko
PUBLISHING

**PUBLISHED BY**
PeKo Publishing Kft.
8360 Keszthely, Bessenyei György utca 37.
Email: infp@pekobooks.com
www.pekobooks.com

**AUTHOR**
Ian Michael Wood

**FIRST PUBLISHED**
2015

ISBN 978-615-80072-7-6

# CONTENTS

★ ★ ★

## SS-Rank Hierarchy and British Equivalents

| **Officer** | |
|---|---|
| SS-Oberstgruppenführer | General |
| SS-Obergruppenführer | Lieutenant General |
| SS-Gruppenführer | Major General |
| SS-Brigadeführer | Brigadier |
| SS-Oberführer | None |
| SS-Standartenführer | Colonel |
| SS-Obersturmbannführer | Lieutenant Colonel |
| SS-Sturmbannführer | Major |
| SS-Hauptsturmführer | Captain |
| SS-Obersturmführer | Lieutenant |
| SS-Untersturmführer | $2^{nd}$ Lieutenant |

| **Non-Commissioned Officer and other Grades** | |
|---|---|
| SS-Sturmscharführer | Sergeant Major |
| SS-Standarten-Oberjunker | None |
| SS-Hauptscharführer | Battalion Sergeant Major |
| SS-Oberscharführer | Company Sergeant Major |
| SS-Standartenjunker | None |
| SS-Scharführer | Sergeant Major |
| SS-Unterscharführer | Sergeant |
| SS-Rottenführer | Corporal |

# INTRODUCTION

★ ★ ★

THIS SHORT HISTORY OF *I./SS-PANZER-REGIMENT 3* began as a short appendix to an ongoing work concerning the *3. SS-Panzer-Division 'Totenkopf'*, but over the years as I researched *I./SS-Panzer-Regiment 3*, I decided to try to complete a history of the *Panther-Abteilung* instead.

Much of the information contained in this short history is new and, with this in mind, any mistakes or misunderstandings are mine alone. I would like to say thank you to Mrs Wood who doesn't understand the term Panzer or Panther, but allowed me the time and space to research this subject.

**Ian Michael Wood,**
UK 2014

# CHAPTER 1

★ ★ ★

## SS-Panzer-Abteilung 4(III) and I./SS-Panzer-Regiment 3

On 8 August 1942, Hitler approved the formation of a *Panzer-Abteilung* for the '*Totenkopf' Division*. The order was backdated to 5 March 1942 on a separate order which authorised a *Panzer-Abteilung* for the '*Das Reich' Division*. On 8 April 1942, the *SS-FHA* (*SS-Führungshauptamt*/ SS Supreme Command Office) issued instructions calling for the formation of three *SS-Panzer-Abteilungen* (armoured units) which was followed up on 18 April 1942 with the *SS-FHA* Abt/Org order 2310/42 geh., setting out the organization and structure of the new *Panzer-Abteilungen. SS-Panzer-Abteilung III* was to be composed of a *Stab* (K.St.Nr. [*Kriegsstärkenachweisung*/Wartime Table of Organization Number] 1107) and a *Stabskompanie* (K.St.Nr. 1150), two *leichte Panzer-Kompanien* (K.St.N. 1171), a *mittlere Panzer-Kompanie* (K.St.Nr. 1175) and a *Werkstatt-Zug* (K.St.Nr. 1185).

On 20 April 1942, the original *Panzer-Abteilung* which had been established for the '*Totenkopf' Division* was reassigned to the '*Das Reich' Division* and designated *SS-Panzer-Abteilung* '*Das Reich*', while the original *SS-Panzer-Abteilung* '*Das Reich*', which had been formed on 11 February 1942, had been reassigned to the '*Wiking' Division* as of 18 April 1942. A new *SS-Panzer-Abteilung* was formed on 20 May 1942 for the '*Totenkopf' Division* and designated *SS-Panzer-Abteilung 4* with an establishment date of 1 June 1942 (note that in some documents *SS-Panzer-Abteilung III* does appear).

On 1 June 1942, the first recruits assembled at the Weimar-Buchenwald Barracks. The new *Abteilung* commander was *SS-Sturmbannführer* Leiner, *SS-Obergruppenführer* Theodore Eicke's son in law. Panzer crew training was conducted at *Panzertruppenschule Putlos* under the command of *SS-Obersturmführer* Kanth, while the *Werkstatt* mechanics were trained at *Panzertruppenschule Wünsdorf* under the command of *SS-Obersturmführer* Eisele.

*SS-Oberscharführer* Steiger recalled*:*

*'In the summer we assembled outside the town of Weimar. The barracks at Buchenwald housed both the Signals and Panzer Schools, and both are linked by a road that's one kilometre long which passes through a beautiful forest.'*

*SS-Unterscharführer* Feichtner reported:

*'In June 1942 I received my transfer to* SS-Panzer-Abteilung III *near Weimar. We had no platoon leaders, so as a young sergeant I was given the honour of being a platoon leader in our Panzer unit. What did we expect? We had no Panzers just a collection of old cars, scrap and some captured Allied tanks. The greater part of the* Abteilung *had been sent on training courses, while I along with the* Werkstatt-Zug *under the command of* SS-Untersturmführer *Eisele [TFK/* Technischer Führer für das Kraftfahrwesen/*technical leader of vehicle engineering] had been sent on a course to* Panzertruppenschule *at Wünsdorf for technical training. We had Alios Mooslechner posted from the* Panzerjäger-Abteilung*, some of the men in the* Panzer-Abteilung *knew him already from their time with the* Panzerjäger-Abteilung*, but within time we got to know him as well.'*

On 1 June 1942 the command structure was as follows.

| | |
|---|---|
| *Abteilungskommandeur*: | *SS-Sturmbannführer* Leiner |
| *Stabskompanie*: | *SS-Obersturmführer* Friedrich |
| *Abt.-Arzt*: | *SS-Hauptsturmführer* Dr Mulich |
| *Hilfsarzt*: | *SS-Obersturmführer* Dr Reithmeyer |
| *TFK*: | *SS-Obersturmführer* Eisele |
| *1/SS-Panzer-Regiment 3*: | *SS-Obersturmführer* Mooslechner |
| *2/SS-Panzer-Regiment 3*: | *SS-Obersturmführer* Kanth |
| *3/SS-Panzer-Regiment 3*: | *SS-Hauptsturmführer* Gross |

On 24 June 1942, another 156 recruits reported to Weimar-Buchenwald after being transferred from the troop training grounds at Debica; soldiers from the *Polizei-Division* were also transferred to *SS-Panzer-Abteilung 4(III)*. The following month, in July 1942, the *Panzer-Aufklärungszug* (tank reconnaissance platoon) was formed and this was commanded by *SS-Untersturmführer* Quade. Meanwhile the training *Panzer-Kompanie* at Putlos, under the command of *SS-Obersturmführer* Kanth, began a tank gunnery course which involved theory and practical target practice.

At the end of August 1942, the *Abteilung* was transported to Mailly-le-Camp in France and then moved onto Suippes near Charlon-sur-Marne. In Suippes, the personnel of *SS-Panzer-Abteilung 4(III)* were issued their black Panzer uniforms.

On 22 September 1942, at a conference with Himmler, Hitler authorised the formation of *Panzer-Regimenten* for the following divisions, '*Leibstandarte*', '*Das Reich*' and '*Totenkopf*'.

*SS-Oberscharführer* Steiger reported on the move to Suippe:
*'Suippe was a small training ground near Chalon which is well known for its monument of the Unknown Soldier and lies on the main road to Chalon.'*

*SS-Unterscharführer* Feichtner reported:
*'Our nice warm days in Weimar were over and we were transferred to La Braconne in France. We have been told that these barracks are pleasant.'*

*SS-Oberscharführer* Steiger reported:
*'In August 1942 some of the crew members came from the* StuG.-Batterie *of the* 'Totenkopf' Division *and others were convalescents recovering from their wounds. Because of their experience with armoured vehicles, these men were distributed amongst the* Kompanien. SS-Oberscharführer *Seifert and* SS-Unterscharführer Fumke *were sent to the regimental* Stabskompanie *as Panzer commanders. SS-Sturmmann Stettner was posted to the* Panzer-Aufklärungszug *as a Panzer commander. Stettner had been the gunner in Meierdrees' Stug., while SS-Sturmmänner Prenzel, Schulze and Sternart were posted to* 1. *and* 2. Kompanie *as Panzer commanders. The rest of the* Stug.-Batterie *was integrated into the new* Sturmgeschütz-Abteilung. *Former Batterie commander,* SS-Hauptsturmführer *Richter was made a* Kompanie-Chef *in the* Panzer-Regiment.*'*

The formation of the new *II. Abteilung* had already begun with the establishment of *5.* and *6. Kompanien* at Weimar-Buchenwald in July. *SS-Panzer-Abteilung 4(III)* was ordered to move to Angouleme on 24 September 1942. During its stay in Suippe, the personnel of the *Abteilung* conducted night exercises and formation training. During October 1942 those '*Totenkopf*' divisional units stationed in France were reassembled in the area of Angouleme and Mailly le Camp; this move involved 22 rail transports, while a further 33 rail transports brought the remaining divisional elements from the Soviet Union between October and November 1942.

On 12 October 1942, *1. Kompanie* of the *Abteilung* received its first delivery of Panzers consisting of one Panzer III *Befehlswagen* (command vehicle), 11 Panzer IIIs with 5cm guns and three with short-barrelled 7.5cm guns, and three Panzer IVs. This equipped the *2. Zug* in *3. Kompanie*.

On 12 October 1942, the *Abteilung* was quartered in La Braconne near Angouleme; on 14 October 1942 *SS-Hauptsturmführer* Meierdrees was appointed commander of the new *I./SS-Panzer-Regiment 3*, the former *SS-Panzer-Abteilung 4(III)*. Meierdrees had previously served in the *StuG.-Batterie 'Totenkopf'* in Russia. After recovering from wounds sustained in Russia, he attended a *Panzer-Abteilung* commander's course before joining *I./SS-Panzer-Regiment 3*.

On 14 October 1942 the command structure of the *Abteilung* was as follows:

*Abteilungskommandeur*: *SS-Hauptsturmführer* Meierdrees
*Adjutant*: *SS-Obersturmführer* Altermüller
*Panzer-Aufklärungszug*: *SS-Untersturmführer* Quade
*1./SS-Panzer-Regiment 3*: *SS-Obersturmführer* Mooslechner
*2./SS-Panzer-Regiment 3*: *SS-Obersturmführer* Kanth
*3./SS-Panzer-Regiment 3*: *SS-Hauptsturmführer* Gross

At the end of October 1942, the first large-scale exercise took place on a training area 3km long. During the drill most of the Panzers broke down due to manufacturing faults. The officers returned to Angouleme after completing company and platoon-leader courses.

On 1 November 1942 the command structure was as follows:

*Abteilungskommandeur*: *SS-Hauptsturmführer* Meierdrees
*Adjutant*: *SS-Obersturmführer* Altermüller
*Ordonnanz-Offizier*: *SS-Hauptsturmführer* Dr. Krogh-Christoffersen
*IVa**: *SS-Untersturmführer* Wolf
*IVb (Artz/*doctor): *SS-Hauptsturmführer* Dr. Mulich
*Nachrichten-Offizier***: *SS-Obersturmführer* Korse
*TFK*: *SS-Obersturmführer* Eisele
*Stabskompanie*: *SS-Obersturmführer* Friedrich
*Panzer-Aufklärungszug*: *SS-Untersturmführer* Quade
*1./SS-Panzer-Regiment 3*: *SS-Obersturmführer* Mooslechner
*2./SS-Panzer-Regiment 3*: *SS-Obersturmführer* Kanth
*3./SS-Panzer-Regiment 3*: *SS-Hauptsturmführer* Gross

* Officer responsible for provisions and equipment.
** Intelligence officer.

In early November 1942 *SS-Obersturmführer* Kanth was ordered to Fallingbostal to oversee the formation of a Tiger tank company designated the *4. (schwere) Kompanie*. The first personnel for this *Kompanie* arrived on 26 December 1942. The

*2. Kompanie* was taken over by *SS-Obersturmführer* Flohr after *SS-Obersturmführer* Kanth took command of the new *4. (schwere) Kompanie*.

On 7 November 1942, *1. Kompanie* was attached to *Kampfgruppe B* as part of *Eingreifgruppe 'Totenkopf'* (a rapid-response unit) during the occupation of Vichy France (*Operation 'Anton'*).

At the end of November 1942, the regimental *Stabskompanie*, and *2.* and *3. Kompanien* were finally equipped with 19 Panzer IIIs and seven Panzer IVs.

On 15 November 1942, the *4. (schwere) Kompanie* was officially formed with crew training on the Tiger conducted under the supervision of *s.Pz.Abt. 502*. On the same day, *SS-Hauptsturmführer* Gross was transferred to *SS-Panzer-Regiment 1* and *3. Kompanie* was taken over by *SS-Hauptsturmführer* Nerpel.

On 19 November 1942, a small number of personnel from *2. Kompanie* of *I./SS-Panzer-Regiment 3* were transferred to *5. Kompanie* of *II./SS-Panzer-Regiment 3*.

On 20 November 1942, *3. Kompanie* received a new intake of trained radio operators while radio operators from the *Panzer-Aufklärungszug* from the *Stabskompanie* were sent on a four-week training course on the Panzer III. On the same day, *SS-Hauptsturmführer* Meierdrees finally assumed command of *I./SS-Panzer-Regiment 3* after completing a *Panzer-Abteilung* commander's course at Wünsdorf which took place between 26 October 1942 and 14 November 1942. Between 6 December 1942 and 30 December 1942, *SS-Untersturmführer* Quarenghi assumed temporary command of *1. Kompanie*.

By 25 December 1942, *1. Kompanie* had returned to Angouleme. In Bergen-Fallingbostel on 1 January 1943, 10 new Panzer IIIs arrived for the *4. (schwere) Kompanie* and on the same day, the *Abteilung* received a new allocation of optics for its Panzers. While at Fallingbostel, *4. (schwere) Kompanie* conducted its first field exercise with their Panzer IIIs on 2 January 1943.

On 8 January 1943, personnel from the *Panzer-Aufklärungszug* of the *Stabskompanie*, under the command of *SS-Untersturmführer* Quade, were transferred to *4. (schwere) Kompanie* and arrived in Fallingbostel on 9 January 1943. The reformed *Panzer-Aufklärungszug* (reconnaissance platoon) of the *Stabskompanie* was now under the command of *SS-Untersturmführer* Lummitsch.

As of 20 February 1943 the command structure of the *Abteilung* was as follows:

| | |
|---|---|
| *Abteilungskommandeur*: | *SS-Hauptsturmführer* Meierdrees |
| *Adjutant*: | *SS-Obersturmführer* Altermüller |
| *Ordonnanz-Offizier*: | *SS-Untersturmführer* Herbatschek |
| *Kraderkundungszug*: | *SS-Untersturmführer* Horstmann |
| *Stabskompanie*: | *SS-Hauptsturmführer* Grams |
| *Stabsscharführer*: | *SS-Hauptscharführer* Pohl |

| | |
|---|---|
| *IVa:* | *SS-Untersturmführer* Wolf |
| *Panzer-Aufklärungszug*: | *SS-Untersturmführer* Lummitsch |
| | |
| *1./SS-Panzer-Regiment 3*: | *SS-Obersturmführer* Riefkogel |
| *2./SS-Panzer-Regiment 3*: | *SS-Obersturmführer* Flohr |
| *3./SS-Panzer-Regiment 3*: | *SS-Hauptsturmführer* Nerpel |
| *4. (s.)/SS-Panzer-Regiment 3*: | *SS-Hauptsturmführer* Mooslechner |
| leichte Kolonne: | *SS-Untersturmführer* Holler |

On 30 January 1943 a detachment was transported by rail to collect 9 new Tigers before returning to Fallingbostel on 7 February 1943. On 1 February 1943, *SS-Panzer-Regiment 3* took delivery of 26 Panzer IIIs. From this batch two Panzer III *Befehlswagen* were issued to *I./SS-Panzer-Regiment 3*. On 3 February 1943, *1. Kompanie* was loaded onto rail transport in the area of Ruelle for deployment to the Soviet Union where it unloaded in Poltava on 14 February 1943.

On 9 February 1943, *2. Kompanie* and the *Stabskompanie* departed Angouleme and arrived in Poltava on 18 February 1943 followed by *3. Kompanie* which arrived in Poltava on 19 February 1943 having departed 11 February 1943. The *4. (schwere) Kompanie* left Fallingbostel on 10 February 1943 and it too arrived in Poltava on 19 February. On 27 February 1943, nine Panzer IV tanks with short-barrelled 7.5cm guns arrived at station in Poltava for *SS-Panzer-Regiment 3* – four of these tanks were collected by *3. Kompanie*.

The *I./SS-Panzer-Regiment 3* fought throughout late February and March 1943 in the battle to retake Kharkov and the capture of Bjelgorod.

On 30 March 1943, *SS-Obersturmführer* Riefkogel was nominated for the Knight's Cross of the Iron Cross for his actions during the night of 16/17 March 1943. Between April and June 1943 the *Abteilung* underwent a period of rest and refitting. On 7 May 1943, *SS-Untersturmführer* Bruno Wolf, the *IVa* for *I./SS-Panzer-Regiment 3*, was made the *IVa* for *SS-Panzer-Regiment 3* until 25 April 1944 when he was transferred to the *21. Waffen-Gebirgs-Division der SS 'Skanderbeg'* on 18 May 1944. He had been the *IVa* for the *Abteilung* since 1 November 1942. The *4. (schwere) Kompanie* was transferred to *II./SS-Panzer-Regiment operation3* and redesignated *9. Kompanie* of *SS-Panzer-Regiment 3* on 9 May 1943.

On the same day the Tiger company's Panzer IIIs were handed over to *3. Kompanie*. A new *4. Kompanie* was formed on 9 May 1943 with *SS-Obersturmführer* Eckl in command and allocated *Feldpost Nr. 57182*. The *Kompanie* personnel were drafted from the disbanded *SS-Kradschützen-Regiment 'Thule'* (disbanded 19 April 1943) and existing personnel from *I./SS-Panzer-Regiment 3*. The *Kompanie* received 14 Panzer IVs on 1 June 1943.

The *1. Kompanie* of the *Abteilung* retained its Panzer IIIs and *2.* and *3. Kompanien* were both equipped with Panzer IIIs; the *2. Zug* of both *Kompanien* had five Panzer IVs each.

On 5 July 1943, *I./SS-Panzer-Regiment 3* took part in *Operation 'Zitadelle'* (Battle of Kursk). On 29 July 1943, *I./SS-Panzer-Regiment 3* collected 13 Panzer IVs from a total of 30 Panzer IVs handed over from *SS-Panzer-Regiment 1.*

From the end of July 1943, the *Abteilung* fought on the Mius line until early August 1943 and later in the same month it was transferred back to the Kharkov area. When the *Abteilung* unloaded, *1.* and *2. Kompanien* were formed into a single *Kampfgruppe* under the leadership of *SS-Obersturmführer* Burgschulte; *3.* and *4. Kompanie* formed a second *Kampfgruppe* under the command of *SS-Obersturmführer* Altermüller. On 11 August 1943, *SS-Obersturmführer* Altermüller was killed in action and the second *Kampfgruppe* was taken over by *SS-Obersturmführer* Herbatschek.

The commander of the first *Kampfgruppe*, *SS-Obersturmführer* Burgschulte, was killed in action on the same day; this *Kampfgruppe* was then taken over by *SS-Obersturmführer* Riefkogel who suffered his seventh wound, again on the same day. After losing both *Kampfgruppe* commanders, the *Abteilung* combined both *Kampfgruppen* into a single *Kampfgruppe* under the command of *SS-Obersturmführer* Herbatschek.

This *Kampfgruppe* was then placed under the command of *SS-Untersturmführer* Strobl, who had recently assumed the position of *Adjutant* on 10 August 1943, when *SS-Obersturmführer* Herbatschek was wounded. The position of *Adjutant* was filled by *SS-Obersturmführer* Heckl who had been transferred from *SS-Panzer-Regiment 2.*

On 18 August 1943, *SS-Untersturmführer* Strobl was wounded and was eventually transferred to *SS-Panzergrenadier-Ausbildungs- und Ersatz-Bataillon 3.* On 15 February 1944, Strobl was ordered to transfer to *I./SS-Panzer-Regiment 3* in Grafenwöhr where he arrived on 18 February 1944.

On 20 August 1943, *SS-Hauptsturmführer* Meierdrees was wounded after being shot in the lung. The *I./SS-Panzer-Regiment 3* was now commanded by *SS-Hauptsturmführer* Säumenicht. Between the 28 June 1943 and 30 June 1943, the *Organisationsabteilung/Generalstab des Heeres* issued two orders requiring *I./SS-Panzer-Regiment 3* to begin conversion training on the Panther tank by the 20 September 1943 and to be in Grafenwöhr by 1 October 1943.

On 21 September 1943, the *I./SS-Panzer-Regiment 3* was assembled in and around Poltava for entrainment to Grafenwöhr for conversion training on the new Panther tank.

Martin Steiger recalled:

*'At a location near Poltava we assembled for entraining back to Germany. We met the other units of the* Abteilung. *Soon we were moved onto another location,*

*and here we received the following order: "The* I. Abteilung *is to be withdrawn and returned to Germany for re-organisation". Some personnel are withdrawn from the combat sections and used as replacements for losses sustained by the* II. Abteilung.*'*

Ludwig Feichter reported:

*'It's difficult to say goodbye to old comrades who do not come with us back to Grafenwöhr for re-organisation. After a fortnight we arrive in Grafenwöhr at night by rail, some of the rail journey took us through Romania. After being discharged I got cleaned up and had a good night's sleep. Upon returning to Grafenwöhr after leave I was moved from* 1. Kompanie, *to the newly formed* 4. Kompanie *were I became the Technical Sergeant;* 4. Kompanie *was filled up with new recruits.'*

In Poltava about 50% of the surviving personnel were transferred to the *II./SS-Panzer-Regiment 3* to replenish losses sustained by the *Abteilung*. The *Versorgungs-Kompanie* (supply company) for the *I./SS-Panzer-Regiment 3* was transported back to Germany as separate unit and arrived in Grafenwöhr on 3 October 1943.

The *TFK* for the *Abteilung*, *SS-Hauptsturmführer* Klemme, was ordered on 27 September 1943 to arrange the transportation of the wheeled vehicles. The wheeled elements of the *Abteilung* were loaded in Kremenchug and after waiting two days rail transport finally crossed the Dniepr River and departed on 29 September 1942 to arrive in Grafenwöhr on 7 October 1943. The train travelled through Alexandria–Kriwoj Rog–Kishinev–Jassy–Budapest–Vienna before finally arriving in Grafenwöhr.

# CHAPTER 2

★ ★ ★

THE I./SS-PANZER-REGIMENT 3 IN 1944

## 2.1. FORMATION AND TRAINING

DURING OCTOBER 1943, *SS-HAUPTSTURMFÜHRER* SÄUMENICHT temporarily led the *Abteilung* until *SS-Hauptsturmführer* Meierdrees had recovered from his wound. Meierdrees assumed command of the *Abteilung* on 20 January 1944. On 13 October 1943, *SS-Hauptsturmführer* Meierdrees was awarded the Oak Leaves to the Knight's Cross.

On 1 November 1943 Heinz Wilhelm Guderian, *Generalinspekteur der Panzertruppen* (Inspector General of the Armoured Troops), had planned to reissue 71 Panthers returned by *I./SS-Panzer-Regiment 1* but this plan was quickly dropped. New recruits from the *SS-Ausbildungs- und Ersatz-Bataillon* based at the Heinrich Himmler Barracks in Prague were transferred to Grafenwöhr to join *I./SS-Panzer-Regiment 3* on 1 December 1943. Most of these new recruits had just completed their Reich Labour Service.

Martin Steiger recalled:

*'All of us took well-earned leave and we all received five pounds of flour, a jar of honey, sunflower oil, all issued from the rations store. After this we went on leave.'*

On 3 December 1943, a *Generalinspekteur der Panzertruppen Führervortag* reported that the issue of 76 Panthers scheduled for *I./SS-Panzer-Regiment 3* (with a handwritten 'W' next to it) were actually issued to *II./SS-Panzer-Regiment 5*.

On 23 December 1943 the first four Panthers were allocated to the *Abteilung* and transported by rail on 1 January 1944.

On 19 December 1943 *SS-Obersturmführer* Lummitsch assumed command of *4. Kompanie* and on 25 December 1943, *SS-Hauptsturmführer* Riefkogel and *SS-Untersturmführer* von Rennenkampf rejoined the *Abteilung* with Riefkogel assuming command of *1. Kompanie* again.

In December 1943 crew training for the Bergepanther (salvage vehicles based on the Panther chassis and equipped with a powerful winch) began and wasn't completed until June 1944. As of 31 December 1943, the *Abteilung* had a strength of 27 officers, 173 NCO's and 800 OR's.

On 15 December 1943, *SS-Untersturmführer der Reserve* Vieweg assumed command of the *Flak-Zug* for *I./SS-Panzer-Regiment 3* after being transferred from the *SS-Flak-* . He had originally been appointed to *I./SS-Panzer-Regiment 3* on 10 October 1943. On 10 January 1944 he attended a further *Flak-Lehrgang* at the *SS-Flak-Ausbildungs- und Ersatz-Regiment* (training and reserve regiment) in Munich and returned to *I./SS-Panzer-Regiment 3* on 26 July 1944. *SS-Untersturmführer der Reserve* Vieweg had originally transferred from the *Schutzpolizei* to the *Waffen-SS* on 10 February 1943 as a commissioned officer (*Leutnant der Reserve*) and was re-commissioned in the *Waffen-SS* as an *SS-Untersturmführer der Reserve.*

**1 JANUARY 1944**

The first four Panthers were dispatched by rail to the *Abteilung* in Grafenwöhr. During January, personnel replacements arrived via the *Panzer-Ersatz-Abteilung* – some of the new crews were destined for the *2. SS-Panzer-Division 'Das Reich'.*

During January 1944, *SS-Oberscharführer* Eggert and *SS-Unterscharführer* Köster returned to *1. Kompanie* after recovering from wounds. *SS-Oberscharführer RFA* (*Reserveführeranwarter*) Wunsch returned after completing the 1st *SS-Panzer-Junker Sonderlehrgang* at Putlos; later in January he was posted back to the *II./SS-Panzer-Regiment 3* and promoted to *SS-Untersturmführer der Reserve* on 4 March 1944. *SS-Obersturmführer* Schramm (posted in on the same day) was appointed as the *Zugführer* (platoon leader). *HalbZugführern* (section leaders) for *1. Kompanie* were as follows: *SS-Oberscharführer* RFA Wunsch, *SS-Oberscharführer* Ober and *SS-Oberscharführer* Baumeister. At this time *1. Kompanie* had a strength of only 50 men.

**10 JANUARY 1944**

*SS-Standartenjunker* Ruscheinski attended the 2nd *SS-Panzer-Junker Sonderlehrgang (III Lehrgruppe)* at Fallingbostel; he reported his presence there on 20 November 1943 and completed the course on 5 April 1944. The *SS-Panzer-Ausbildungs- und Ersatzund Ersatz-Regiment* based at Weimar reported that, as of 1 April 1944, he was to be assigned to *I./SS-Panzer-Regiment 3*. Ruscheinski was promoted to *SS-Standartenjunker* on 1 March 1944. On 21 June 1944 he was promoted to *SS-Untersturmführer* and then posted to the *SS-Panzer-Ausbildungs- und Ersatz-Regiment* where remained until 28 February 1945.

## 13 JANUARY 1944

The first four Panthers arrived and each *Kompanie* was issued a single Panther for training purposes. The *Abteilung* in terms of manpower was now at full strength.

Martin Steiger recalled:

*'After leave was completed, the* Abteilung *reassembled, and we were surprised to see* SS-Sturmbannführer *Meierdrees again (he had been recently promoted to* Sturmbannführer*) in our midst. This time he was wearing the Oak Leaves to the Knight's Cross and gave a short address to the men. Riefkogel was still recovering from his wounds in a Hospital in Berlin; we were still awaiting his return to the* Kompanie. SS-Hauptsturmführer Säumenicht was award*ed the Knight's Cross for his actions on 2 September 1943. After Christmas the* Kompanie *received its first officer,* SS-Untersturmführer *von Rennenkampf. Next to return was* SS-Hauptsturmführer *Riefkogel who finally took command of the* Kompanie. *We had around 50 men on strength; it would take another 50 or so men to bring the* Kompanie *up to full strength. Just after the New Year, the first rail transport arrived, bringing new replacement personnel. To our surprise, on this transport were some old comrades who had recovered from their wounds.*

*Among the Panzer commanders who returned to us were Eggert and Köster,* SS-Oberscharführer *Wunsch returned after completing an officer training course at the Cadet School in Braunschweig. Further replacements arrived via the* SS-Panzer-Ersatz-Abteilung*; these new replacements were originally meant for the* 'Das Reich' Division. *The* Kompanie *was now at full strength and* Hauptsturmführer *Riefkogel started a full training program at the end of January 1944.*

*With snow on the training grounds, this left something to be desired. The barracks were of the sort our grandfathers occupied – not very inviting. Another officer arrived at the* Kompanie, *this was* SS-Obersturmführer *Schramm. Later,* SS-Untersturmführer *Kaden arrived as well, and because of his youth we gave him the nickname Budi'.*

SS-Oberscharführer *Wunsch, Ober and Baumeister were made half-platoon leaders in the* Kompanie, *the* Kompanie Spiess (sergeant) *was Guido Eck. The senior mechanic in the* Kompanie *was Erich Fleuter and vehicle section-leader was Lochmann. Eric Fleuter had two assistants who helped with administration and welfare; they were Karrer and Katzfey. The* Kompanie *was rebuilt within a very short period of time, this counted for the rest of the* Abteilung *as well, and this meant that we could return to the* Division *which was still fighting in the east.'*

## 20 JANUARY 1944

*SS-Hauptsturmführer* Meierdrees returned after recovering from his wounds and assumed command of *I./SS-Panzer-Regiment 3*. The *Abteilung* began radio and signals training; the course commander was *SS-Oberscharführer* Schaller and *SS-Untersturmführer* Connert the senior instructor. The signals officer during this period was *SS-Obersturmführer* Quierling. The first group to go through the course came from the *Stabskompanie* (Headquarters Company). New recruits were also given training on the Panther tank turret and bow machine-gun systems. During late January and February 1944, training on the Panther tank was limited due to chronic fuel shortages.

### 21 JANUARY 1944

The *SS-FHA* ordered the transfer of *SS-Obersturmführer* Bormuth from the *SS-Panzer-Ausbildungs- und Ersatz-Regiment* at Sennelager to *I./SS-Panzer-Regiment 3* based at Grafenwöhr. This order also instructed *SS-Obersturmführer* Bormuth to report to *I./SS-Panzer-Regiment 3* by 1 February 1944.

### 30 JANUARY 1944

*SS-Hauptsturmführer* Meierdrees was promoted to the rank of *Sturmbannführer*. During January 1944, *SS-Untersturmführer* Borkmann was transferred to *SS-Wachbataillon 5* as their new *IVa* officer. *SS-Untersturmführer* Stege assumed the post of *Ordonnanz-Offizier* (ordnance officer) for *I./SS-Panzer-Regiment 3*, while *SS-Obersturmführer* Bormuth was promoted to *SS-Hauptsturmführer*.

### 31 JANUARY 1944

*Generalinspekteur der Panzertruppen* scheduled the *I./SS-Panzer-Regiment 3* to be fully equipped by 25 March 1944 and ready for deployment by 10 April 1944.

From 1 February 1944 to 12 February 1944, the officers of the *Abteilung* attended courses at the *Panzertruppenschule Putlos*.

During February 1944 the trainee radio operators and gunners developed the skills necessary for handling their new charges. The gunners also received limited gunnery practice on the ranges at Grafenwöhr. *SS-Hauptsturmführer* Walter Bormuth was officially posted to *I./SS-Panzer-Regiment 3* and assumed command of *2. Kompanie.* He attended the 15th combined *Panzer-Kompanie Führerlehrgang* at the military training grounds on the Lüneburger Heide (*Truppenübungsplatz Bergen*) between 3 January 1944 and 29 January 1944 and then, from 31 January 1944 to 3 February 1944, attended a gunnery course at the *Panzertruppenschule Putlos.*

Also joining the *Abteilung* at Grafenwöhr was *SS-Untersturmführer der Reserve* Heise who had been transferred from *SS-Panzer-Ausbildungs- und Ersatz-Regiment* at Bitsch. *SS-Untersturmführer der Reserve* Heise had already served with *I./SS-Panzer-Regiment 3* during the battles around Kharkov in February 1943 and at Kursk as a *Zugführer*. From the 21 January 1944 to 12 February 1944, Heise attended a gunnery course at the *Panzertruppenschule Putlos* and *Oldenburg*.

## 7 FEBRUARY 1944

SOME OF THE OFFICERS ATTENDED the *Panther-Lehrgang* course at Erlangen. This course was completed on 12 February 1944. Other courses began on 14 February 1944 but these took place at the Bergen and Putlos. On 7 February 1944, *SS-Obersturmführer* Strobl attended an SS hospital after which he was ordered to report to *I./SS-Panzer-Regiment 3* by the 15 February 1944 but he did not arrive in Grafenwöhr until 18 February 1944.

## 29 FEBRUARY 1944

DUE TO ONGOING DELAYS WITH deliveries, the *Generalinspekteur der Panzertruppen* again rescheduled the timeline for the *I./SS-Panzer-Regiment*, with equipping to be completed by 20 April 1944 and the unit ready for commitment by 5 May 1944.

At the end of February 1944, *SS-Obersturmführer der Reserve* Quilitz returned to *I./SS-Panzer-Regiment 3* after completing the 24th *Kriminalassistent-Lehrgang* (criminal investigators course) at the Security Police School in Fürstenberg. The course began on 1 November 1943 with attendee's being notified only on 20 October 1943, which meant that *SS-Obersturmführer der Reserve* Quilitz, who before the outbreak of war had been a police detective, had to cut short his home leave to report for the course.

## 1 MARCH 1944

BEFORE BEING POSTED TO *I./SS-PANZER-REGIMENT 3*, *SS-Untersturmführer* Leciejewski attended a gunnery course at the *Panzertruppenschule Putlos*, which he completed on 4 March 1944. Leciejewski had served with *1. Kompanie* of *SS-Panzer-Regiment 3* during the earlier part of 1943 before attending a signals course at the SS-Signals School in Nurnberg after which he attended the 1st *SS-Panzer-Junker Sonderlehrgang* at Putlos from the 17 August 1943 to 6 November 1943. He was commissioned on 1 March 1944.

On 4 March 1944, *SS-Untersturmführer* Köster was also posted to *I./SS-Panzer-Regiment 3* after being promoted to *SS-Untersturmführer* on 1 March 1944. Köster had attended the same gunnery course as *SS-Untersturmführer* Leciejewski and had previously served with the *Abteilung* as a dispatch rider in the *Stabskompanie* with the rank of *SS-Sturmmann*. Between the 17 August 1943 and 6 November 1943, he attended the 1st *SS-Panzer-Junker Sonderlehrgang* at Putlos. *SS-Untersturmführer* Leciejewski departed for Grafenwöhr on 5 March 1944 while *SS-Untersturmführer* Köster went on home leave.

*SS-Untersturmführer* Koleczek was also officially posted to *I./SS-Panzer-Regiment 3*. During 1943, he too had attended the 1st *SS-Panzer-Junker Sonderlehrgang* at the *Panzertruppenschule* at Putlos. Koleczek was promoted to *SS-Untersturmführer der Reserve* on 1 March 1944 and attended the same gunnery course at Putlos as Leciejewski and Köster before departing for Grafenwöhr on 5 March 1944. Koleczek had served with *SS-Infanterie-Regiment 2* from November 1939 to January 1941 and then spent a period of time serving in various *SS-Ersatz Regimenten*. From the 17 April 1943 he served with *3. Kompanie* of *I./SS-Panzer-Regiment 3*. *SS-Hauptscharführer RFA* (*Standartenoberjunker*) Friedrich Mink was promoted to *SS-Untersturmführer der Reserve* on the same day after being posted in from *SS-Panzer-Ausbildungs- und Ersatz-Regiment Bitsch* and took command of the *Pionier-Zug*. Friedrich Mink had also attended the 1[st] *SS-Panzer-Junker Sonderlehrgang (Lehrgruppe III)* from the 17 August 1943 to 6 November 1943. On 1 May 1943 he had been promoted to *SS-Oberscharführer* while serving with *I./SS-Panzer-Regiment 3* as a *Schreinermeister* (master carpenter).

### 3 MARCH 1944

A SECOND DELIVERY OF SIX Panthers arrived in Grafenwöhr giving each *Kompanie* two Panthers for training purposes. On 25 March 1944, it was reported that the *Abteilung* was still missing its allocation of 89 trucks. The *Generalinspekteur der Panzertruppen* expected these trucks to be provided via an exchange with another *SS-Division*.

### 13 MARCH 1944

*SS-UNTERSTURMFÜHRER* KÖSTER REPORTED TO ERLANGEN for the *Panzer-Lehrgang* 'Panther'. He arrived at Erlangen on 12 March 1944 at 1800 hours at the end of home leave. The course was completed on 25 March 1944 after which Köster attended a gunnery course at the *Panzertruppenschule Putlos*; the course lasted from the 27 March 1944 to 1 April 1944.

### 25 MARCH 1944

ACCORDING TO THE *PZ.OFF.F.CHEF.ST.D.HEER*, UPON completion, the factory production for April should have allowed a total of 163 Panthers to be issued to the following units as follows:

> *I./SS-Panzer-Regiment 2* with six Panthers to be issued a further 41 Panthers;
> *I./Panzer-Regiment 'Grossdeutschland'* with four Panthers to be issued a further 56 Panthers;
> *I./SS-Panzer-Regiment 3* with 10 Panthers to be issued a further 66 Panthers.

On the same day, *SS-Hauptsturmführer* Geiling arrived and assumed command of the *Versorgungs-Kompanie*. Geiling had previously served with the *SS-Totenkopf-Standarte Oberbayern* from September 1937 to July 1938, then *SS-Totenkopf-Standarte Ostmark* until September 1940; from September 1940 to February

1943 he attended various SS-officer schools at Bad Tölz and Braunschweig. From February 1943 until October of the same year he served with the *Lettische* (Latvian) *SS-Freiwilligen Brigade*. From 12 October 1943 to 6 November 1943 he attended a course at the *Panzertruppenschule Bergen* and from 8 November 1943 to 13 November 1943 he attended another course at the *Panzertruppenschule Putlos* after which he was posted to the *SS-Panzer-Ausbildungs- und Ersatz-Regiment* until March 1944.

**31 MARCH 1944**

THE *ABTEILUNG* WAS STILL SITUATED in Grafenwöhr under the command of *SS-Sturmbannführer* Erwin Meierdrees. With immediate effect, the *I./SS-Panzer-Regiment 3* was ordered by the *SS-FHA* to be transferred to Arcis-sur-Aube and report to the *Stab* (headquarters) of *Panzer-Brigade 10* (Reims) for further unit training. During March 1944, the *Abteilung* was again experiencing trouble with the supply of new tanks.

The *Generalinspekteur der Panzertruppen* scheduled *I./SS-Panzer-Regiment 3* to be fully equipped by 25 June 1944 and ready for commitment by 10 July 1944. During March, *SS-Untersturmführer* Ksienzik and *SS-Untersturmführer* Gottsching were posted to *I./SS-Panzer-Regiment 3*. Ksienzik had attended the 1st *SS-Panzer-Junker Sonderlehrgang* from 17 August 1943 to 6 November 1943 along with *SS-Untersturmführer* Gottsching. Both had been promoted to the rank of *Untersturmführer* on 1 March 1944.

Martin Steiger reported:

*'However there are difficulties in the delivery of Panther tanks. Each Kompanie has two or three Panzers for training use. A larger issue of Panzers was initially thought of but cancelled. We have to load up and move to France on 1 April 1944 – we must make space for a larger* Wehrmacht *unit.'*

**1 APRIL 1944**

THE *I./SS-PANZER-REGIMENT 3* WAS ENTRAINED in Grafenwöhr for rail transport to France. Upon arrival, some of the troops were quartered at La Braconne, where *I./SS-Panzer-Regiment 3* was issued its first Panzers during 1942.

**10 APRIL 1944**

THE *I./SS-PANZER-REGIMENT 3* REPORTED TO the Staff of *Panzer-Brigade 10* at Mailly-le-Camp. Various training detachments were sent to the *Panther-Lehrgang* in Erlangen for training courses with transport via Sedan. At the end of April 1944, by order of *Generalinspekteur der Panzertruppen*, *I./SS-Panzer-Regiment 3* handed over five Panthers to *SS-Panzer-Regiment 1*. These five Panthers were collected at Mailly-le-Camp by a collection command from *SS-Panzer-Regiment 1* between 12 May 1944 and 13 May 1944.

**15 APRIL 1944**

*SS-Obersturmführer* Klemme, *TFK* for *I./SS-Panzer-Regiment 3*, attended a vehicle technical course from the 15 April 1944 to 21 May 1944. *SS-Obersturmführer* Klemme had served with *SS-Infanterie-Regiment 4* from April 1941 until March 1942 when he was transferred to the *SS-Panzer-Ersatz-Kompanie.* On 14 March 1942 he attended a vehicle technical course in Vienna before being posted to *SS-Panzer-Abteilung III.*

**20 APRIL 1944**

*SS-Untersturmführer der Reserve* Quilitz, signals officer of *I./SS-Panzer-Regiment 3*, was promoted to *SS-Obersturmführer der Reserve.*

**24 APRIL 1944**

*SS-Untersturmführer der Reserve* Steinegger attended a gunnery course at Celle which he completed on 15 May 1944. Steinegger had attended the 1st *SS-Panzer-Junker Sonderlehrgang* at Putlos from the 17 August 1943 to 6 November 1943 and was promoted to the rank of *Untersturmführer der Reserve* on 1 March 1944.

**25 APRIL 1944**

*SS-Untersturmführer* Bruno Wolf had previously served with *I./SS-Panzer-Regiment 3* from 1 November 1942 to 7 May 1943 when he was appointed *IVa* of the regiment. He was then transferred to the Albanian *21. Waffen-Gebirgs-Division der SS 'Skanderbeg'* on 18 May 1944.

On 30 April 1944, the *Generalinspekteur der Panzertruppen* issued a new schedule for *I./SS-Panzer-Regiment 3* which stated that equipping was to be complete by July 1944 and the regiment ready for deployment by August 1944.

Between 1 May 1944 and 15 May 1944, some of the officers of *I./SS-Panzer-Regiment 3* attended a *Zugführer* course – this had been arranged by *Inspektion 6 (Panzertruppen)* of the *SS-FHA* – for the Panther tank at the *Panzertruppenschule Bergen.* The following officers attended the course:

*SS-Obersturmführer der Reserve* Quilitz, Alfred (SS-Nr 54-681), *Stabskompanie;*
*SS-Untersturmführer der Reserve* Schramm, Eric (SS-Nr 120-109), *1. Kompanie;*
*SS-Obersturmführer* Herbatschek, Roman (SS-Nr 421-049), *3. Kompanie;*
*SS-Obersturmführer* von Kleist, Lothar (SS-Nr 423-810), *4. Kompanie;*
*SS-Untersturmführer der Reserve* Heise, Helmut (SS-Nr 287-939), *2. Kompanie;*
*SS-Standartenoberjunker der Reserve* Schäfer, Georg (SS-Nr 69-059), *2. Kompanie.*

During the night of 3 May 1944 and the early morning hours of 4 May 1944, Mailly-le Camp was attacked by 250 Lancaster bombers of the R.A.F. in a raid that lasted 30 minutes. The camp was seriously damaged but the personnel of *I./SS-Panzer-Regiment 3* survived without serious casualties although *I./Panzer-Regiment 35* (*4. Panzer-Division*) suffered 44 dead. The R.A.F. lost 42 Bombers during the raid.

Martin Steiger reported:

*'By May we are staying in this lovely but somewhat boring place. Our* Kompanie-Chef *and* Zugführern *are on a course at the* Panther-Lehrgang *in Erlangen but the* Abteilung *is ordered to re-allocate to Sedan.'*

**5 MAY 1944**

*SS-Hauptsturmführer* Säumenicht was transferred to *SS-Panzer-Regiment 5* and on 19 May 1944 took over effective command of *I./SS-Panzer-Regiment 5.*

*SS-Obersturmführer* Lummitsch, the commander of *4. Kompanie*, conducted search and patrol operations around Mailly-le-Camp and it was during one of these operations that his soldiers came under attack by US fighter-bombers. Fortunately for them, *4. Kompanie* did not sustain any losses during this action.

**22 MAY 1944**

*SS-Hauptscharführer* Dr. Wolf Gunther Abt was posted to the *Panther-Abteilung* as the new doctor. *SS-Hauptscharführer* Dr. Abt had been transferred from the *Luftwaffe* on 3 May 1944 and became a member of the *Waffen-SS* on 17 June 1944. He was made an officer cadet with the rank of *SS-Standartenoberjunker der Reserven* and promoted to *SS-Untersturmführer der Reserve* on 1 August 1944.

### Status Report 1 May 1944, *I./SS-Panzer-Regiment 3*

(Under the command of *Panzer-Brigade 10*)

| Manpower | Authorized / Shortfall |
|---|---|
| Officers | 33 / 3 |
| NCOs | 364 / 15 |
| Other ranks | 679 / 31 |
| Total | 1076 / 49 |

Replacements: two officers and two NCOs and other ranks
Casualties from 1 April 1944 to 30 April 1944: one dead, one hospitalized

| Vehicles | Authorized/Operational/In repair |
|---|---|
| Panzer V Panther | 76 / 4 / 1 |
| SPW | 5 / - / - |
| Kettenkrad* | 6 / - / - |
| Motorcycle w/sidecar | 1 / 1 / 1 |
| Motorcycle | 28 / 13 / 1 |
| Cars (off road) | 54 / 3 / 1 |
| Cars (on road) | - / 2 / - |
| Maultier (half-track) | 7 / 5 / 1 |
| Truck (off road) | 95 / 3 / - |
| Truck (on road) | 15 / 29 / 3 |
| Prime Mover (1-5t) | 9 / - / - |
| Prime Mover (8-18t) | 14 / - / - |
| RSO | - / - / - |

* Kettenkrad (tracked motorcycle)

| Weapons | Authorized / Available |
|---|---|
| Rifles | 510 / 510 |
| Pistols | 476 / 476 |
| Sub-MG | 114 / 110 |
| MG 34 | 169 / 34 |
| 2cm Flak | 3 / - |
| 7.5cm KwK | 76 / 5 |

*Commander's Comments*

*Status of Training:*

*With the return of those elements that attended the* demonstration *team at Erlangen on 30 April 1944, the greater part of the training of the* Abteilung *has been completed.*

*On 6 May 1944, within the* Abteilung*, the individual training on the Panther will be completed. By the following week, platoon training should commence and this will be finished by the end of May.*

*Status of Equipment:*

*By order of the* Generalinspekteur der Panzertruppen, *the* Abteilung *with 10 Pz Vs on hand, has had to hand over five Pz Vs to* 1. SS-Panzer-Division L.A.H. [Leibstandarte Adolf Hitler] *just as the* Abteilung *was about to begin platoon training. The inventory of five Pz Vs is not sufficient, nor satisfactory for future training at platoon level.*

*A new delivery of wheeled vehicles has not yet arrived. The vehicles brought back with the* Abteilung *have been ready since November 1943 after a complete overhaul in various maintenance depots and need transportation.*

*There is a protracted shortage of spare parts and specialised vehicles. With the current training and organisation, the scarcity of workshop vehicles is particularly noticeable. The moral and health of the troops is good.*

*Signed, Meierdrees*

*Panzer-Brigade 10* Commander's *Comments:*

*In agreement with the valued judgement of the* Abteilungskommandeur.

*The tank one-on-one training for combat crews and combat sections is mostly complete. Presently, crew training is at platoon level and the performance so far is satisfactory. With only five Pz Vs on hand, this is not ideal for training purposes – a new allocation of at least five Pz Vs would be reasonable for future platoon training. The shortage of spare parts for repairs is* affecting *further proposed combat training.*

*Signed, Oberst Streit,* Kommandeur Regiment-Ausbildungs-Stab

## 5 JUNE 1944

Both *SS-Untersturmführer* Koleczek and *SS-Untersturmführer der Reserve* Oevermann attended the 2nd Chemical Warfare Course at Bromberg, completing it on 22 June 1944. Oevermann, like many of the new officers posted into *I./SS-Panzer-Regiment 3*, had attended the 1st *SS-Panzer-Junker Sonderlehrgang* at Putlos, being promoted to *Untersturmführer der Reserve* on 1 March 1944.

## 6 JUNE 1944

The *1. Kompanie* of the *I./SS-Panzer-Regiment 3* was transported to Pynei near Troyes for security duties where it spent most of June 1944. During the time spent in Pynei, *SS-Hauptsturmführer* Riefkogel had the *Kompanie* conduct infantry field excerises. During early June 1944, *Generaloberst* Guderian inspected the troops stationed in Mailly-le-Camp. Later he attended a gathering of officers amongst whom was *SS-Sturmbannführer* Meierdrees. At this meeting Guderian expressed the view that an Allied invasion of France, if successful, could end Germany's cause and the lose them the war.

**10 JUNE 1944**

*SS-Obersturmführer* Kuhner arrived and became the new TFW (*Technischer Führer Waffenwesen*/ Chief Technical Weapons Officer) of the *Abteilung*. Kuhner had previously served at the *SS-Waffen-Techinscher-Lehranstalt* (SS-Weapons Technical Establishment) in Dachau.

**11 JUNE 1944**

The schedule issued by the *Generalinspekteur der Panzertruppen* for *I./SS-Panzer-Regiment 3* required it to be equipped by July 1944 and ready for commitment by 15 August 1944. About this time, two officers from Skorzeny's unit appeared in Mailly-le-Camp trying to recruit members of the *I./SS-Panzer-Regiment 3* to join *SS-Fallschirmjäger-Bataillon 500* but were promptly told to leave and not to return. *SS-Sturmbannführer* Meierdrees called Hitler's headquarters to inform them of his dipleasure at the recent visit of the two officers and at the same time raised the issue of the shortfall in the number of Panthers in his unit.

*SS-Oberscharführer* Steiger recalled his time spent in France:

'*Current status of the unit: training is proceeding and has reached an advanced stage and as such we can expect a new delivery of tanks at any time, even during the night. Night alarms are not a rarity, but the guard has been doubled. The French are very busy expecting the imminent aid of the Americans. The resistance groups attack German troops and commit acts of sabotage – the rest of the country is simmering underneath. Currently we are in a awkard situation and are awaiting a very important order. At present we do not know when we will be deployed but rumours spread from mouth to mouth and the current thought is that we will be going soon. The accomodation in Pynei near Troyes has a very peaceful location and training can proceed undisturbed so that progress is better than expected. We still have to carry out infantry excerises from platoon upto company level – these are carried out across the open terrian using infantry weapons and machine guns. At night, some of the more courageous men venture out to get extra rations such as meat which is put into the soup. Riefkogel knows nothing of what is going on but Guido Eck, who knows the ration distribution system, has an idea although Riefkogel is still at a loss. Some of the Sisters from the Soldiers Home deliver cakes and coffee which again improves the ration quota. Lately officers, NCO's and OR's have gone into the fields picking fruit, but due to the situation Riefkogel has to impose restrictions on the movement in and out of the village. Suddenly, the order we have all been waiting for arrives. Panzer collection parties are organised and sent to Breslau and Magdeburg to collect the remaining Panzers which will fill out the* Kompanien.

### 12 JUNE 1944

*SS-Untersturmführer der Reserve* Mink attended a *Lehrgang für Offiziere im Truppenpionierdienst* at the *Pionierschule Thorn* (based at the Ulanen-Kaserne) which he completed on 8 July 1944.

### 21 JUNE 1944

*SS-Untersturmführer* von Kleist was promoted to *Obersturmführer* and *Untersturmführer der Reserve.* Heise was promoted to *Obersturmführer der Reserve.* Also *SS-Standartenjunker* Ruscheinski was promoted to the rank of *SS-Untersturmführer* (see entry for 10 January 1944).

### 23 JUNE 1944

A collection detachment was sent to *Heereszeugamt Breslau-Masselwitz* and *Magdeburg-Königsborn* to collect the new Panthers. Between the months of April and June 1944 – since the arrival of *I./SS-Panzer-Regiment 3* in Mailly-le-Camp – the *Abteilung* had spent a great deal of time chasing elements of the French Underground with little to show for their efforts which led to it acquiring the nickname of 'Meierdree's Flying Circus'.

## Status Report, 1 June 1944, *I./SS-Panzer-Regiment 3*

(Under the command of *Panzer-Brigade 10*)

| Manpower | Authorized / Shortfall |
|---|---|
| Officer | 36 / 3 |
| NCO | 358 / 8 |
| Other ranks | 683 / 26 |
| Total | 1077 / 37 |

Replacements: two officers and two NCOs or other ranks
Convalescents: one
Casualties 1 May 1944 to 1 June 1944: six hospitalized, two others sick.
*(Note: two of the six casualties in hospital were injured during training accidents.)*
Absent on training courses for 12 to 18 months: one man

| Vehicles | Authorized /Operational/In repair |
|---|---|
| Panzer V Panther | 76 / 3 / 2 |
| SPW | 5 / - / - |
| Kettenkrad | 6 / - / - |
| Motorcycle w/ sidecar | - / 1 / - |
| Motorcycle | 28 / 13 / - |
| Cars (off road) | 54 / 3 / - |
| Cars (on road) | 1 / 1 / - |
| Maultier (half-track) | 7 / 5 / 1 |
| Truck (off road) | 104 / 2 / 1 |
| Truck (on road) | 8 / 30 / 6 |
| Prime Mover (1-5 t) | 14 / - / 2 |
| Prime Mover (8-18 t) | 14 / - / - |
| RSO | - / - / - |

| Weapons | Authorized /Available |
|---|---|
| Rifles | 516 / 510 |
| Pistols | 559 / 575 |
| Sub-MG | 124 / 98 |
| MG 34 | 124 / 98 |
| MG 42 | 152 / 9 |
| 2cm Flak | 3 / 3 |

*Commander's Comments:*

*At present the* Abteilung *has five Pz Vs on hand; another five that* have *been allocated have not yet arrived. The stock of wheeled vehicles on strength is still unchanged. Since the last status report, about 50% of the vehicle stock is still in the HKP and needs transporting.*

*Due to transport problems the maintenance vehicles could arrive any week but as yet a new allocation has not taken place. As regards personnel, the* Abteilung *and pioneer platoon are at full strength.*

*The Abteilung is still conducting platoon training and target practice with MG and main gun. The shortage of tanks, fuel and training ammunition has significantly impaired skill levels.*

*Signed, Meierdrees*

*Panzer-Brigade 10* Commander's *Comments:*

*I agree with the* Abteilungskommandeur. *The* Abteilung *has had to carry out external security duties in the HML area of Troyes and this has reduced training by eight to ten days. Training has therefore been stepped up.*

*Signed, Kappenburg*

## Status Report, 1 July 1944, *I./SS-Panzer-Regiment 3*

(Under the command of *Panzer-Brigade 10*)

| Manpower | Authorized/Shortfall |
|---|---|
| Officer | 34 / 1 |
| NCO | 353 / - |
| Other ranks | 597 / - |
| Total | 984 / 1 |

Casualties 1 June 1944 to 1 July 1944: none
Replacements: none
Absent for 12-18 months: one man

| Vehicles | Authorized/Operational/In repair |
|---|---|
| Panzer V Panther | 76 / 6 / 4 |
| Bergepanthers | 2 / 2 / - |
| SPW | 5 / - / - |
| Kettenkrad | 16 / - / - |

*Continued from previous page*

| Vehicles | Authorized/Operational/In repair |
|---|---|
| Motorcycle w/sidecar | - / 1 / - |
| Motorcycle | 5 / 12 / 2 |
| Cars (off road) | 37 / 2 / - |
| Cars (on road) | 1 / - / - |
| Maultier (half-track) | 8 / 6 / - |
| Truck (off road) | 96 / 2 / 1 |
| Truck (on road) | 4 / 27 / 5 |
| Prime Mover (1-5 t) | 9 / - / 2 |
| Prime Mover (8-18 t) | 10 / - / - |
| RSO | - / - / - |
| Trailer | 8 / 2 / - |

| Weapons | Authorized/Available |
|---|---|
| Rifles | 420 / 512 |
| Pistols | 414 / 574 |
| Sub-MG | 109 / 103 |
| MG 34 | 152 / 9 |
| MG 42 | 25 / 17 |
| 2cm Flak | 3 / 3 |

*Commander's Comments:*

*The* Abteilung *now has 10 Pz V and two Berge-Pz Vs; another allocation of 10 Pz Vs has not yet arrived. 50% of vehicles are still in the HKP, maintenance but vehicles are* en route. *A new allocation of vehicles that was due has still not arrived.*

*Personnel levels in the* Abteilung *and pioneer platoon are at full strength. The Abteilung is still conducting platoon training. On the gunnery range, at least three KwK main guns have been used during target practice.*

*Again, fuel shortages for tactical training are still affecting training. Regarding the supply of ammunition – no problems or difficulties.*

*Signed, Meierdrees*

*Panzer-Brigade 10* Commander's *Comments:*
*I agree with the* Abteilungskommandeur; *there is a slim chance of larger-scale training exercises but only if more fuel is released.*

*Signed, Kappenburg*

**Officer Positions Stand 1 July 1944**

| | |
|---|---|
| *Abteilungskommandeur*: | *SS- Sturmbannführer* Meierdrees |
| *Adjutant*: | *SS-Obersturmführer* Strobl |
| *Ordonnanz-Offizier*: | *SS-Untersturmführer* Stege |
| *Nachrichten-Offizier*: | *SS-Obersturmführer der Reserve* Quilitz |
| *IVa:* | *SS-Obersturmführer* Spieker |
| *IVb:* | *SS-Hauptscharführer* Dr. Abt (*SS-Standartenoberjunker der Reserve*) |
| *TFK*: | *SS-Obersturmführer* Klemme |
| *Werkmeister*: | *SS-Untersturmführer der Reserve* Reitwiessner |
| *TFW**: | *SS-Obersturmführer* Kuhner |
| *Panzer-Pionierzug*: | *SS-Untersturmführer der Reserve* Mink |
| *HalbZugführer*: | *SS-Unterscharführer* Kreutzer |
| *Gruppenführer*: | *SS-Unterscharführer* Pahl und *SS-Rottenführer* Hainbach |
| *Panzer-Aufklärungszug*: | *SS-Obersturmführer* Rudolph |
| *Flak-Zug*: | *SS-Untersturmführer der Reserve* Vieweg |
| *Stabskompanie*: | *SS-Obersturmführer* Nadel |

**TFW* (*Technischer Führer für das Kraftfahrwesen)*/engineering officer responsible for transportation)

**1./ SS-Panzer-Regiment 3:**

| | |
|---|---|
| Commander: | *SS-Hauptsturmführer* Riefkogel |
| *Kp.-Spiess*: | *SS-Hauptscharführer* Eck |
| | *SS-Obersturmführer* Schramm |
| | *SS-Untersturmführer* von Rennenkampf |
| | *SS-Untersturmführer* Kaden |
| | (*SS-Oberscharführer* Wunsch) |

**2./ SS-Panzer-Regiment 3:**

| | |
|---|---|
| Commander: | *SS-Hauptsturmführer* Bormuth |
| | *SS-Obersturmführer der Reserve* Heise |
| | *SS-Untersturmführer der Reserve* Schäfer |
| | *SS-Untersturmführer* Köster |

**3./ SS-Panzer-Regiment 3:**

| | |
|---|---|
| Commander: | *SS-Hauptsturmführer* Zech |
| | SS-Obersturmführer Herbatschek |
| | *SS-Untersturmführer* Gottsching |
| | *SS-Untersturmführer* Koleczek |

**4./ SS-Panzer-Regiment 3:**

| | |
|---|---|
| Commander: | *SS-Obersturmführer* Lummitsch |
| *Kp.-Spiess*: | *SS-Oberscharführer* Rudolf |
| | *SS-Obersturmführer* Retzdorf |
| | *SS-Obersturmführer* von Kleist |
| | *SS-Untersturmführer der Reserve* Oevermann |
| *Versorgungs-Kompanie*: | *SS-Hauptsturmführer* Geiling. |

### 4 JULY 1944

The schedule of the *Generalinspekteur der Panzertruppen* for *I./SS-Panzer-Regiment 3* required it to have been equipped by 10 July 1944 with a commitment date – logged by the *Generalinspekteur der Panzertruppen* – as 25 July 1944.

### 5 JULY 1944

*SS-Untersturmführer* Ruscheinski was transferred back to the *SS-Panzer-Ausbildungs- und Ersatz-Regiment* after completing the 3rd *Oberfähnrichlehrgang der Panzertruppen* at Gross-Glienicke.

### 7 JULY 1944

The *I./SS-Panzer-Regiment 3* was ordered (*Generalinspekteur der Panzertruppen*, Abt.Org.Nr. 1909/44 g.k., 7 July 1944) to Grafenwöhr to complete equipping with Panthers. The remaining vehicle allocation was supervised by *Wehrkreis XIII*.

### 10 JULY 1944

OKH/St.d.H/Org.Abt Nr I/18009 g.kdos. reported that *I./SS-Panzer-Regiment 3* was to be operationally ready between 20 July 1944 and 24 July

1944 along with *I./Panzer-Regiment 27* of the *19. Panzer-Division*. On the same day, *SS-Hauptsturmführer* Balzer assumed command of *2. Kompanie* after completing the 19th *Panzer-Abteilung* Commander's Course, which ran from 30 May 1944 to 8 July 1944. *SS-Hauptsturmführer* Balzer had served with the *SS-Panzerabwehr-Abteilung* of the *SS-Verfügungsdivision* from 9 November 1939 to 1 March 1940, when the *SS-Verfügungsdivision* was renamed *SS-Division 'Reich'*. He served with *SS-Regiment 'Deutschland'* until 1 July 1942. From 1 July 1942 to 10 July 1944 he served with the *SS-Panzerjäger-Ersatz-Abteilung* before attending a course at the *Panzertruppenschule Putlos* between 27 March 1944 and 1 April 1944. The former *2. Kompanie Chef*, *SS-Hauptsturmführer* Bormuth, left *I./SS-Panzer-Regiment 3* and was transferred to *1. Kompanie* of *SS-Panzer-Regiment 12* where he took over from *SS-Hauptsturmführer* Berlin.

**14 JULY 1944**

The *I./SS-Panzer-Regiment 3* commenced loading onto two rail transports in readiness for departure to Grafenwöhr in Germany.

**15 JULY 1944**

The *I./SS-Panzer-Regiment 3*, which was already loaded onto two rail transports in Mailly-le-Camp, departed for Grafenwöhr in Germany.

**16 JULY 1944**

The *I./SS-Panzer-Regiment 3* arrived in Grafenwöhr from Mailly-le-Camp. The long-awaited delivery of trucks also arrived in Grafenwöhr. A small collection party had gone to the Saurer factory in Vienna and returned with new Saurer 5-ton trucks including spare parts for the vehicles.

Martin Steiger reported:

*'We arrive back in Grafenwöhr again; the entire Abteilung is to be supplied in the shortest time with new Panther tanks. The joy with the new Panther is immense; we conduct some short* Kompanie *exercises which means we are to redeploy soon. Many women came to Grafenwöhr so they can spend the last days with their men. For many months leave has been cancelled for the whole* Abteilung. *So many relatives came to Grafenwöhr to say goodbye.'*

**17 JULY 1944**

A report by *Armeeoberkommando 4* detailing the tank situation for *3.SS-Panzer-Division 'Totenkopf'* shows *I./SS-Panzer-Regiment 3* with 50 Panthers on hand. The new Panthers were delivered with a yellow undercoat; camouflage and turret numbers were applied to the new tanks in Grafenwöhr. According to statements by veterans, the *Abteilung* received about 20 model Ausf. G Panthers the remainder being Ausf. A models.

**19 JULY 1944**

ORDERS (ORG./OP. ABT. 8333/44 GEH.) were issued for *I./SS-Panzer-Regiment 3* to be transported by rail to re-join the *3. SS-Panzer-Division 'Totenkopf'*, which was now under the command of *Heeresgruppe Mitte*. Loading for the first transport commenced from midday onwards but spent the night in the rail yards and did not depart until 22 July 1944. On the same day, *SS-Untersturmführer* Werner Mittag was posted to the *Abteilung* and arrived at Grafenwöhr where he was assigned to the *Panzer-Pionierzug*. *SS-Untersturmführer* Mittag had just completed the 2nd *SS-Panzer-Junker Sonderlehrgang* (special training course) at Fallingbostel which ran from the 25 April 1944 to 8 July 1944.

**20 JULY 1944**

OKH/ST.D.H/ORG.ABT. NR I 18028 G. kdos., reported that *I./SS-Panzer-Regiment 3* would be ready for deployment between the 25 July 1944 and 31 July 1944. Also listed as being ready or deployed were *I./Panzer-Regiment 15* and *I./Panzer-Regiment 27*.

**21 JULY 1944**

THE LAST DELIVERY OF PANTHERS and *mittlere* SPWs (Schützenpanzerwagen/armoured vehicle) arrived at Grafenwöhr.

**22 JULY 1944**

THE FIRST RAIL TRANSPORT LEFT Grafenwöhr for *Heeresgruppe Mitte*. *Generalfeldmarschall* Model was informed that the *Abteilung* was *en route* with 78 Panthers. Of this total, three Befehlspanther (command tanks) and two other Panthers were handed over to the regimental *Stabskompanie* of *SS-Panzer-Regiment 3* upon arrival.

## 2.2. DEPLOYMENT

### Overview

*OPERATION 'BAGRATION'* WAS THE CODENAME for the Soviet offensive designed to clear German forces under the command of *Heeresgruppe Mitte* out of Belorussia. The offensive began on 22 June 1944 and almost destroyed the German *4. Armee*, *3. Panzerarmee* and *9. Armee*. The German response was to rebuild a new front in central Poland to stem the Soviet onslaught. Within this framework, the *3. SS-Panzer-Division 'Totenkopf'* was ordered to move from Romania to Poland. Entraining began on 8 July 1944 and *I./SS-Panzer-Regiment 3* was instructed to return to its parent division.

### 24 JULY 1944

At 2230 hours the first rail transport arrived with eight Panthers at the eastern railway station in Warsaw. Unloading was carried out under cover of darkness to avoid the threat of a Soviet air attack. At 0005 hours on 25 July 1944, the first seven Panthers formed an advance party with motorised elements of the *II./ Grenadier-Regiment 170* of the *73. Infanterie-Division.*

At 0105 hours on 25 July 1944, the advance party left Warsaw for Siedlce, entering the town at 0400 hours. At 0255 hours the *XX. Armeekorps* was informed that *1. Kompanie* and the reinforced truck-mounted *II./Grenadier-Regiment 170* (with about 450 men) from the *73. Infanterie-Division* was to be deployed in the area of Siedlce. Two Panthers remained behind in Wengrow and would later re-join the *Abteilung* on 26 July 1944 along with six other wheeled vehicles.

At 2345 hours on 24 July 1944, the second transport arrived with 10 Panthers and began unloading. As early morning approached on the 25 July, one Panther remained on its rail flatcar. During the day, the first rail transports bringing the *Fallschirmjäger-Panzer-Division 'Hermann Göring'* also began arriving from Italy. At 2335 hours the *Ia* for *Heeresgruppe Mitte* informed the *Ia* (*Erste Generalstabsoffizier* /1st General Staff Officer) of *Armeeoberkommando 2* that the first rail transport had arrived and that another 70 Panthers were expected.

During this period *SS-Oberscharführer* Steiger wrote:

*'Our transport arrived in Warsaw without any trouble; we began unloading sometime around midnight. The* Panther-Abteilung *was incorporated back into the T-Division. Orders issued to the* Panther-Abteilung *stated that we had to reach Siedlce as quickly as possible as the Russians were threatening to break through our lines. It was an 80km march from Warsaw to Siedlce. We moved just after midday in the searing heat and reached the edge of Siedlce around 1500 hours. When we got there we saw fleeing soldiers, female communication operators and civilian workers all racing west. Also in the crowd were* Organisation Todt *and railway workers. As they passed us some shouted insults at us while others offered words of good luck. Siedlce appeared to be clear of any German soldiers and we soon got word that Russian tanks had been spotted. We halted in the town centre and the* Kompanie-Chef *issued orders "A German Staff group is trapped in Brest-Litowsk; the Abteilung will advance with 1. Kompanie at point". The attack began at 2000 hours heading in a south-easterly direction with SS-Obersturmführer Schramm's platoon at point.*

*The Russians had set up strong defensive positions along a railway line. Very quickly the lead Panther was knocked out, it was commanded by SS-Oberscharführer Ober. The Panther of SS-Untersturmführer von Rennenkampf was also put of action. The* Kompanie *did manage to destroy two T-34 tanks. The attack was a failure so we had to return to Siedlce.'*

Also *SS-Sturmmann* Richter recalled:

*'It was midnight when we arrived and the unloading was conducted in complete darkness as the Russians were flying at night looking for targets. Also arriving in Warsaw were our comrades from the* Hermann Göring Division, *they came from Italy. As the sun came up in the morning, we realised that a Panther was still sitting on its rail flatcar. Before long we got the order to prepare to march towards Siedlce.'*

The tank drivers had received very little training in loading/unloading procedures during a rail move and this caused a lack of confidence in handling their new charges. In Siedlce the Germans had prepared three armoured trains to aid the defence of the town.

**25 JULY 1944**

By 0730 hours, another four rail transports had arrived in Warsaw's eastern railway station. At 0725 hours in Siedlce, *SS-Hauptsturmführer* Riefkogel talked by phone to *Oberst* Lassen, the *Ia* for *Armeeoberkommando 2*. Riefkogel reported that until he received 7m$^3$ fuel he could not move his Panthers. He further complained to *Oberst* Lassen that the local military authority had refused to supply the material. *Oberst* Lassen asked *SS-Hauptsturmführer* Riefkogel how many Panthers had already been moved. Riefkogel replied that five Panthers had been moved but that he still needed fuel for the rest. *Oberst* Lassen then asked Riefkogel how long it took to drive to Siedlce from Warsaw, to which Riefkogel replied that it took three hours to travel the 90km.

By 0930 hours a total of six rail transports had been unloaded. At midday, 43 Panthers had assembled and these were ordered to proceed to Siedlce with 25 of them arriving during the late afternoon, followed by another six a little later.

At 0635 hours the following day, the battle commander for Siedlce reported that the first 10 Panthers had been a great help and had already knocked out six or seven Soviet tanks. At 0725 hours only five Panthers remained operational with another five requiring a new allocation of fuel.

At 0825 hours, another five Panthers rolled into Siedlce. At 0830 hours the *Ia* of the *73. Infanterie-Division* reported that one *Panther-Kompanie* and all of *II./Grenadier-Regiment 170* were in place. The five Panthers without fuel received a new allocation between 1030 and 1045 hours.

In Siedlce, *SS-Hauptsturmführer* Riefkogel assembled the platoon leaders for briefing. Soviet tanks had been reported east of Siedlce and Soviet artillery was already shelling parts of the town. Meanwhile, at 1327 hours the last two rail transports arrived in Warsaw east railway station carrying the last elements of the *Abteilung*. These Panthers left Warsaw at 1530 hours.

At 1955 hours, 20 Panthers were deployed for an attack on Miedzyrec with *Obersturmführer* Schramm's platoon leading the attack. The point tank – commanded by *SS-Oberscharführer* Ober from *1. Kompanie* – encountered strong Soviet anti-tank gunfire from the reverse slope of a railway embankment. Ober's Panther took a direct hit and caught fire. The leader of the 2nd platoon, *SS-Untersturmführer* von Rennenkampf, was wounded when his Panther was hit but the rest of his crew managed to escape. The attack was called off and *1. Kompanie* returned to Siedlce leaving in the in the fields near the rail embankment seven immobile Panthers, three of which were bogged down and awaiting recovery. Later that night, elements of *I./SS-Panzer-Regiment 3* were in combat near Golice until the early hours of the 26 July 1944. Also on 25 July 1944, *SS-Hauptsturmführer* Geiling was placed in command of the Panzer regiment's vehicle supply *Kompanie* which was composed mainly of the former *Versorgungs-Kompanie* of *I./SS-Panzer-Regiment 3*. The *Abteilung* therefore had to organize another *Versorgungs-Kompanie* from existing vehicles stocks and issued it with a new *Feldpost* number. *SS-Untersturmführer* Kaden was placed in command of this unit. The third platoon of *1. Kompanie* was taken over by *SS-Oberscharführer* Wunsch.

## 26 JULY 1944

During the morning, the *I./SS-Panzer-Regiment 3* reported that seven Panthers damaged the previous evening were awaiting recovery for repairs to battle damage; three of these were stuck in a cornfield.

At 0900 hours, the last two transports arrived in Warsaw carrying the *Panzer-Werkstattzug* and the other wheeled elements. At 1950 hours, 20 wheeled vehicles left the *Panzer-Werkstattzug* in Warsaw for Siedlce; six more wheeled vehicles followed on at 2000 hours. Also leaving Warsaw for Siedlce were 32 wheeled vehicles of the newly organised *Versorgungs-Kompanie*. Meanwhile, the unloading of *I./SS-Panzer-Regiment 3* was completed.

The *1. Kompanie* with 20 Panthers was assembled and placed under the command of *SS-Sturmbannführer* Meierdrees with orders to operate under the command of the *VIII. Armeekorps*. Attached to *Kampfgruppe Meierdrees* were two *Kompanien* of *Panzergrenadiere*. The mission of this battle group was to outflank the Soviets. The *SS-Totenkopf Division* requested the return of this *Kampfgruppe* by 0245 hours on 27 July 1944. For this mission, the *VIII. Armeekorps* issued 300 7.5cm armour-piercing KwK (Kampfwagenkanone/mobile battle cannon) shells and 100,000 rounds of 7.92mm belt ammunition. The Panthers advanced on Mordy and then pushed on to Losice and Miedzyrec to enter Mszanna during the early morning hours of the 27 July. The *1. Kompanie* was situated in the woods north-west of Mszanna. Due to the situation in Siedlce, the *'Totenkopf'* divisional command requested the Panthers to return to divisional control at 0150 hours on 27 July 1944. *Kampfgruppe Meierdrees* then had to fight its way back through Mordy to re-enter Siedlce, destroying 11 Soviet tanks in the process.

While the bulk of *I./SS-Panzer-Regiment 3* was under the command of *SS-Hauptsturmführer* Riefkogel, he was given orders to free up the roads around Mordy. Riefkogel planned to use *3. Kompanie* to advance along the road to Miedzyrec while *2. Kompanie* advanced northwards on Borki and thereafter north-eastwards to Golice. Elements of *4. Kompanie* (minus a single platoon) were to attack south-west towards Skozec. Later, the *XX. Armeekorps* reported that all the attacks had been repelled by strong fire from Soviet tanks and anti-tank guns. During the attack, the crew of *SS-Oberscharführer* Kessler was reported missing but another report stated that Panther 124, Kessler's tank, had been hit and that he and the gunner, Erich Koser, had been badly wounded when their tank was knocked out. Siedlce came under heavy Soviet artillery fire during which *SS-Unterscharführer* Massari, *SS-Sturmmann* Koser and *SS-Sturmmann* Robel were killed by shell splinters as they took cover underneath a Panther tank. During the day, a Panther from *3. Kompanie* was repaired after being hit by anti-tank fire which damaged the main gun. *SS-Obersturmführer* Heise from *2. Kompanie* was killed during the fighting near Borki – his Panther was struck by several anti-tank rounds.

A Panther commander also wrote:

*'The situation in completely unsure – the Russians have crossed the highway to the north-west near Mordy where the Hungarian troops are based.'*

*SS-Rottenführer* Lindau of *3. Kompanie* wrote:

'SS-Hauptsturmführer *Riefkogel explained that we had to break through to relieve the troops in Miedzyzrec. The advance would begin in the evening. The commander of Panther 333 was* SS-Unterscharführer *Picha, the gunner was myself and the loader was an 18-year-old. The driver was* SS-Rottenführer *Wendland and the radio operator was Jupp Hille. We stopped for a short time during which a Russian anti-tank gun fired two rounds at our turret, these shells bounced off our Panther. When this happened I had my note book out which dropped into the interior of the tank. After some initial panic we gathered ourselves and found the anti-tank gun which we promptly destroyed. The Panther of* SS-Unterscharführer *Burcher needed repair due to damage on the Panther's main gun*'.

*SS-Obersturmführer* Lummitsch was wounded during the fighting in Riakla; *SS-Obersturmführer* Retzdorf took command of *4. Kompanie* which had been tasked with covering the main road from Warsaw to Siedlce and took up positions west and north-west of Siedlce. On this hectic day a small number of Panthers had to deal with the Soviet 20th Tank Brigade as it advanced from the south-east, engaging them in Bialka and also to the south-east, near Chromna.

## 27 JULY 1944

During the day, the *Abteilung* remained inactive due to ongoing fuel shortages. A new allocation of fuel was promised during the afternoon. *1. Kompanie* served as the divisional reserve while the bulk of the *Abteilung* moved into the area of Mszanna. In Siedlce, seven Panzer IVs from *7. Kompanie* conducted a limited counterattack to the west of the town, escorted by 200 *Grenadiere.* Later, six Panzer IVs were reported in the town. During the day, *SS-Obersturmführer* Lummitsch was evacuated from the divisional field hospital to the rear area for further medical treatment.

## 28 JULY 1944

In the afternoon, *Kampfgruppe Meierdrees* reformed with the *Stabskompanie* and *1. Kompanie,* along with two *Kompanie*n from the *III./SS-Panzergrenadier-Regiment 5 'Totenkopf'.* Their task was to advance on Mordy. This *Kampfgruppe* consisted of 23 Panthers. At 1300 hours, *XX. Armeekorps* ordered the completion of the operation by 0100 hours on 29 July 1944. The *Kampfgruppe* set off along the eastern exit road from Siedlce where it came under heavy Soviet artillery fire. As the *Kampfgruppe* advanced towards Stok-Lacki, the Panthers and *Grenadiere* came under strong Soviet defensive fire from heavy weapons and anti-tank guns. Even though the operation was expected to be complete by 0100 hours on 29 July 1944, the ongoing combat situation around Siedlce forced the *Kampfgruppe* to fight its way back to the town during the early morning hours of 29 July 1944. *SS-Hauptsturmführer* Riefkogel was appointed tank defence officer for Siedlce.

During the morning of the 28 July 1944, a Panzer IV and eight Panthers were fighting on the southern outskirts of Siedlce. The roads to the south of Siedlce leading to Zelkow-Kolonia and Zelkow were cut by the attacking Soviet forces and in the afternoon this Panther group withdrew back to Siedlce. In the eastern and south-eastern part of the town, other elements of the Panther-Abteilung were fighting near Grabianow – along the Siedlce-Miedzyrec road leading onto Starowiejska Street – supported by elements of II./Grenadier-Regiment 170 from the 73. Infanterie-Division. As the day wore on, the fighting became centred on the eastern suburbs of the town where parts of III./SS-Panzergrenadier-Regiment 6 'Eicke' were supporting I./SS-Panzer-Regiment 3. The Soviets were now trying to attack Siedlce from both the east and west. By the end of the day, the Panthers in Siedlce were again running short of fuel and nearly half of them required repairs to damage sustained in combat. The TFK, SS-Hauptsturmführer Klemme, was already reporting that the Abteilung desperately needed spare tracks, engines and other parts.

A Panther commander recalled 28 July 1944:
'Although we had almost run out of ammunition and we were down to the last drop of fuel, we had to reach the edge of town and link up with the Grenadiere as the Russians were now fighting for the highway into Siedlce.'

SS-Oberscharführer Steiger recalled:
'After 3 days of combat the company sergeant major, Guido Eck, had to write off large parts of the company as losses. The number of killed and wounded was staggering.'

From the 4. Kompanie, a platoon under the command of SS-Obersturmführer von Kleist was attached to SS-Panzergrenadier-Regiment 6 'Eicke'. The platoon fought in the area of Opole-Stare, 8km west of Siedlce. In the area of Siedlce the Panther-Abteilung, with the assistance of the 7. Kompanie from II./SS-Panzer-Regiment 3, managed to knock out the following Soviet tanks: 10km from Siedlce, near Przygody, seven Soviet tanks were spotted, of which three were knocked out; 3km east of Siedlce a large Soviet motorised column was observed and two Soviet tanks were knocked out while in the woods near Dobrowka-Wylazy two further Soviet tanks were knocked out; at around midday, in the vicinity of Golice, 7. Kompanie with six Panzer IVs knocked out three Soviet tanks 5km north-east of Siedlce,

After SS-Untersturmführer Kaden had been transferred from 1. Kompanie, he finally assumed command of the new Versorgungs-Kompanie. The commander of Panther 424 from 4. Kompanie was wounded along with SS-Panzerschütze Thielecke. Also wounded during the day were SS-Oberscharführer Henschel and SS-Unterscharführer Siefert.

### 29 JULY 1944

Seventeen Soviet tanks which had assembled near Grabianow village, south of Siedlce were met by a guide from the Polish Home Army detachment in Siedlce (this force was made up of 80 volunteers and two German Army deserters). The Soviet commander hoped to push through Siedlce heading north and to capture the Siedlce-Sokolow Podlaski crossroads by attacking towards Zythnia street and then Sokolwska street a manoeuvre that meant crossing a series of marshy fields. The Polish Home Army guide tried to convince the commander of the Soviet tank unit that this was a bad idea but the Soviet officer ignored this warning and at around midday the Soviet tanks tried to advance on Siedlce but fifteen of them quickly became stranded in the waterlogged ground which gave the Panthers and Panzer IVs of *SS-Panzer-Regiment 3* the opportunity to immediately launch a counterattack with the divisional artillery providing covering fire. Of the 17 Soviet tanks, only two managed to escape but one of these was later found abandoned after suffering mechanical failure. A German patrol quickly found the Soviet tank crews and an escort party from the Polish Home Army hiding in the north-western part of the town. German mortar and artillery fire was directed onto their position, killing three and wounding four of the Polish Home Army members. At 1745 hours, the first Soviet tanks entered Siedlce, but these were quickly pushed back by elements of *2.* and *4. Kompanie*. The *Abteilung* knocked out five T-34 tanks and three JS-2 heavy tanks. Also, Panther I04 from the *Stabskompanie* hit and destroyed a T-34 tank during the fighting.

A veteran from the *Panther-Abteilung* recalled:

*'In Siedlce we had no fuel and couldn't drive out of the town. We had 12 Panthers that could not move. The Russians attacked us at 1435hours in the afternoon.'*

*SS-Untersturmführer* Gottsching was wounded after his Panther was hit and damaged by Soviet tank fire. Also wounded during the day was *SS-Untersturmführer der Reserve* Vieweg, the *Flak-Zug* commander for *I./SS-Panzer-Regiment 3*. He was treated in the *'Totenkopf'* divisional hospital on 31 July 1944. The *II./SS-Panzergrenadier-Regiment 6 'Eicke'* took up defensive positions south-west of Siedlce, in the area of Wylazy-Dabrowka. The battalion had a small detachment of Panthers attached to provide support. The *I./SS-Panzergrenadier-Regiment 5 (gepanzert) 'Totenkopf'*, under the command of *SS-Hauptsturmführer* Berg, arrived in Sokolow. This battalion had 700 *Grenadiere*, 80 wheeled vehicles and 20 *mittlere* SPWs. After finally assembling, the battalion marched to Siedlce to provide support for the Panzer IVs and Panthers holding the town. Further west along the highway to Warsaw, the *I./SS-Panzergrenadier-Regiment 6 'Eicke'* defended the Broskow sector while the *III./SS-Panzergrenadier-Regiment 6 'Eicke'* was deployed to the south-east of Siedlce.

## 30 JULY 1944

During the day, the Panthers of *I./SS-Panzer-Regiment 3* were engaged in street fighting with Soviet tanks as their forces tried to enter the town from the west and the east. During the fighting *SS-Hauptsturmführer* Zech, commander of *3. Kompanie*, was wounded and *SS-Obersturmführer* Herbatschek assumed command of *3. Kompanie*. The commander of *4. Kompanie*, *SS-Obersturmführer* Retzdorf, was killed during the day's fighting and *SS-Obersturmführer* von Kleist assumed command of *4. Kompanie*. Meanwhile, *SS-Oberscharführer* Gumbl took over the 3rd platoon of *4. Kompanie*. The motorcycle scout-platoon commander,

*SS-Untersturmführer* Stege (the ordnance officer) was killed during the fighting for Kopice. He was replaced by *SS-Untersturmführer* Steinegger. The Germans relinquished control of Siedlce by 0300 hours on 31 July 1944.

The *I./SS-Panzer-Regiment 3* withdrew to the north, towards Suchozerby. *SS-Unterscharführer* Stadelmeier's Panther from *3. Kompanie* took a hit and caught fire. During the afternoon another Panther group with 18 Panthers, and support by two *Panzergrenadier* battalions, launched a counterattack against the Soviet 3rd Guards Cavalry Division from the western exit of Siedlce along the highway heading towards Warsaw with an attack directed towards Broskow. During the counterattack two Panthers were damaged by Soviet defensive fire. At the western exit of Siedlce, some Panthers provide covering fire for the withdrawing elements of *SS-Panzergrenadier-Regiment 6 'Eicke'* and the *III./SS-Panzer-Artillerie-Regiment 3*. German forces tried to clear the Soviet and Polish Home Army positions centred on Siedlce's Reymenta Street and Cmentarna Street. To the south of Siedlce, the Soviets occupied the eastern edge of Rakowiec and the Germans promptly launched a counterattack but this was repulsed with the loss of six Panthers. From 25 July 1944 to 30 July 1944, the *I./SS-Panzer-Regiment 3* lost 25 Panthers and suffered around 110 casualties.

The driver of Panther I04 wrote:

*'To our front sat a T-34 on the street corner and then it started driving straight towards us, "free fire" ordered the commander,* SS-Oberscharführer *Meier. The shell struck the T-34, spinning the tank on its axis. Some of the crew bailed out and a second T-34 was spotted. We had him in our sights – a round struck the second T-34. White smoke billowed out of the tank. A huge explosion took place sending steel plates up into the sky – a jet of flame shots out of the engine compartment.'*

A Panther commander also remembers:

*'The Russians stop and fire at us, we receive hits to the turret, hull, mantle and the road wheels. Screws and rivets go flying everywhere.'*

*SS-Rottenführer* Lindau recalled:

*'The Panther of* SS-Unterscharführer *Stadelmeier is shot up and catches fire; the* Unterscharführer *is considered a real hero with an excellent reputation. The* Abteilung *commander, SS-Sturmbannführer Meierdrees, awards him the Iron Cross First Class as Stadelmeier lies dying from his wounds'.*

Another Panther crewman wrote:

'To *drive to our new position we had to dig our Panther out. The tracks were having trouble with the muddy ground, it was unpleasant.* SS-Hauptsturmführer

*Riefkogel came to our aid and took up a position with his Panther obliquely to ours, so he could keep an eye on the Russians. He tried to hurry us along as he stood in the cupola of his Panther. Soon we were able to attach the couplings and call Riefkogel over so we could be towed but the Russians opened fire with artillery. A splinter hit me in the knee. I was taken to the regimental field hospital under the command of* SS-Hauptsturmführer *Dr. Schaurmann.'*

SS-Hauptsturmführer Riefkogel was hit by a mortar fragment during a briefing; he died later in the clearing station. SS-Obersturmführer Schramm was then put in command of 1. Kompanie. When Riefkogel was wounded, the Kompanie-Spiess, SS-Hauptscharführer Guido Eck, was present. He reported Riefkogel's words: 'Greetings to my proud Kompanie, from now on SS-Obersturmführer Schramm will lead the Kompanie'.

SS-Oberscharführer Steiger remembered:
'He treated the men of his Kompanie as if they were his own boys.'

**31 JULY 1944**

The *Kompanien* of the *Abteilung* were placed in various locations: *1. Kompanie* was near Suchozerby. By now the technical condition of the *Abteilung* was not good. The six Panthers in long-term repair all had jammed turrets and damage to their, gun mantles, final drives, steering mechanisms, engine covers, hulls and tracks. Those Panthers in short-term repair had suffered light engine and gearbox damage. There was also a shortage of wheels, wheel rims and cylindrical roller bearings. Elements of the *Abteilung*, along with the Panzer regiment, were in action south-west of Okuniew while under the command of *Armeeoberkommando 9*. Of the four new Panthers delivered, one of them was collected by the crew of *SS-Obersturmführer* Schramm of *1. Kompanie*. *SS-Untersturmführer* Rennenkampf, leader of the *2. Zug*, was wounded and replaced by *SS-Oberscharführer* Ober. The platoon of *SS-Obersturmführer* von Kleist returned to *I./SS-Panzer-Regiment 3* after being attached to *SS-Panzergrenadier-Regiment 6 'Eicke'*. During this period the platoon managed to knock out two Soviet anti-tank guns and two Soviet tanks. In the northern part of Siedlce, the *III./SS-Panzergrenadier-Regiment 5 'Totenkopf'*, defended the sector and the road leading to Chodowo.

A Panzer commander reported:
*'We just received an order that we must deploy along the front as Ivan has been seen moving towards our positions with tanks and infantry. We let them approach and have them in our sights. A Tiger is placed on the right of the road and is sheltered by a railway embankment – its gun covers the road to Chodow. The Tiger's turret swivels,*

*his 8.8cm gun fires a round at the lead T-34 tank which is hit. As I move up behind the Tiger, the Panzer of* SS-Unterscharführer *Holtorf fires at the third Russian T-34 tank which catches fire after being hit. Our Grenadiers set to amongst the Russian infantry. Our crew is working as a single man; the ventilator continues to extract the fumes from the turret. Two Russian T-34's are burning. A third Russian T-34 tank is spotted; we fire a round at the tank which hits broadside. We reload our gun and fire at another T-34 tank which is now on fire and enveloped in thick, oily black smoke.'*

The following is an excerpt from the nomination report for the German Cross in Gold for *SS-Obersturmführer* von Kleist, *4. Kompanie*:

*Defensive fighting in the area of Siedlce 25 July -30 July 1944*

*'After the enemy had pushed east, south and south-west of Siedlce, a Russian assault group tried to advance along the main highway from Siedlce to Warsaw and then head north-west of Siedlce. At the time* SS-Obersturmführer *von Kleist and his platoon were attached to* SS-Panzergrenadier-Regiment 6 'Eicke' *from the 28 July 1944 to 31 July 1944. On 28 July 1944,* SS-Panzergrenadier-Regiment 6 'Eicke' *with the attached platoon of* SS-Obersturmführer *von Kleist engaged Russian forces in the area of Opole-Stare, 8km west of Siedlce. The Russians were trying to push south and south-east of Siedlce and long the Siedlce-Warsaw highway with strong infantry and tank forces,* SS-Obersturmführer *von Kleist, without infantry support, managed to push the enemy back and outflank several anti-tank gun positions while coming under strong Russian anti-tank gunfire and mortar fire. During the fighting,* SS-Obersturmführer *von Kleist managed to destroy two Russian tanks and two anti-tank guns and seize several Russian positions. Two of the Panthers, including his own tank, were hit and damaged and* SS-Obersturmführer *von Kleist was lightly wounded while commanding another Panther. With two other Panthers, he engaged and led another counterattack against a Russian tank force during which his platoon came under KW-85 and T-70 gunfire. During this attack von Kleist destroyed several mortar positions and seized the high ground held by the enemy.'*

Excerpt from an eyewitness account by Polish resident of Siedlce, Lucjan Dmowski:

*'When the shooting stopped I returned to the city. Siedlce was an unimaginable desert of ruin and rubble. My house on the corner of Kazimierzowska and Starowiejska Street was just a burnt-out heap of rubble with the chimney still standing upright in the middle of the ruin. My house had caught fire after the Panther tank standing next to it was hit and caught fire. The crew of the Panther had all been killed; you could see the skull of the driver through the open hatch. In the streets of the city lay dead soldiers. A Russian soldier lay in a heap in a gutter near the Post Office while*

*a dead German officer was hanging over the fence that surrounded the Pilsudski memorial. Also lying in the streets were dead, bloated horses which created a stench that was unbelievable. So ended the German occupation only to be replaced by the "Consolidation of the People's Power"– in other words, communist occupation.'*

**1 AUGUST 1944**

The *1. Kompanie* was attached to *I./SS-Panzergrenadier-Regiment 5 'Totenkopf' (gepanzert).*

**2 AUGUST 1944**

Elements of *I./SS-Panzer-Regiment 3* engaged Soviet forces south-west of Mlecin. Other elements of the *Abteilung* encountered the 103rd Soviet Tank Brigade and the 1,295th Self-Propelled Artillery Regiment along the road to Wola Polska. The *Abteilung* claimed one T-34 tank and two armoured cars destroyed but its *IVa* officer, *SS-Obersturmführer* Spieker, was reported missing in action. *SS-Obersturmführer* Oeynhausen, who had originally served with *II./SS-Panzer-Regiment 3*, took over as the new *IVa* officer,

**3 AUGUST 1944**

The *Abteilung* command post was set up in the church in Stanislawow along with a first-aid clearing station to which the wounded were sent for evacuation to the rear. The first postal delivery arrived for the *Abteilung* from Germany – the first post since it left Grafenwöhr.

Between Banachowizna and east of Nadbiel, the bulk of the *Abteilung* assembled in readiness to counterattack the ongoing Soviet thrusts along the Kolno-Zabraniec road. During the afternoon, the Panthers engaged the Soviet 50th Tank Brigade in the area of Reczajc-Zabraniec. Other elements of the *Panther-Abteilung* were deployed in the area of Gorki where they engaged the Soviet 51st and 103rd Tank Brigades. The Panthers were provided with covering fire by anti-tank guns. A single *Panther-Kompanie* from *I./SS-Panzer-Regiment 3* was assigned to *I./SS-Panzergrenadier-Regiment 9 'Germania'*. The *1. Kompanie* of *SS-Panzer-Regiment 3* was located near Stanislawa. Two Tigers from *9. Kompanie* were attached to the *Abteilung* and saw action near Banachowizna and east of Nadbiel as they engaged the Soviet 3rd Tank Corps.

*SS-Oberscharführer* Steiger wrote:

*'After the battle for Siedlce we regrouped at the crossroads in Stanislawow. Here the first post arrives and is distributed. The* Kompanie *cook, Tausch, brings the ration canister with new rations. Due to the heat we wear sports shorts inside the Panzers. The front line is about 1 kilometre away and during the day the Russians fire two*

*shells into the middle of a gathering which kills, Wunsch, Tausch, Scheer, Friedrich and Müller; several others are badly wounded and are quickly evacuated to the field hospital. Schramm and Eck learn of the attack at the command post during a briefing with* SS-Sturmbannführer *Meierdrees. Next to the church in Stanislawow, we bury six comrades who are quietly laid to rest.'*

By the end of the day's action, the Soviet 3rd Tank Corps had lost 78 tanks. The *I./SS-Panzer-Regiment 3* reported no losses.

**4 AUGUST 1944**

Late in the evening, elements of *I./SS-Panzer-Regiment 3* were in the area of Krubki-Gorki; a single *Panther-Kompanie* was attached to *I./SS-Panzergrenadier-Regiment 9 'Germania'* from the *5. SS-Panzer-Division 'Wiking'*. The *Kampfgruppe* advanced on Chobota and Mrowiska. Those elements in Krubki were later involved in action along with elements of the *4. Panzer-Division* in the area north-east of Gorki and Malkow. Three Tigers from *9. Kompanie* were attached to *I./SS-Panzer-Regiment 3* and saw action near Okuniew. The *Stabskompanie* was involved in a counterattack near the woods 1km west of Zalesie.

**5 AUGUST 1944**

The *Panther-Kompanie* from *I./SS-Panzer-Regiment 3* attached to the *5. SS-Panzer-Division 'Wiking'*, saw action in the area of Wolomin.

**10 AUGUST 1944**

The *Panther-Abteilung* was involved in defensive actions as Soviet forces tried to breech the front line of the *3. SS-Panzer-Division 'Totenkopf'*, between Ludwinow and Natolin. The *I./SS-Panzer-Regiment 3* came under heavy Soviet artillery fire and during the day the *Panzer-Aufklärungszug* commander, *SS-Obersturmführer* Rudolph, was killed in action. The *Stabskompanie* saw action south of Pniewnik.

SS-Oberscharführer Steiger reported:

*'The Russian artillery fire is non-stop; this is followed by Russian attacks against our weak front lines. Their material strength is immense, the gaps between our grenadiers is about 100-200 metres each. We are again called forward to the front line; this time the Russians are threatening our supply routes. The Russian attack is supported by tanks. We manage to knock some of their tanks out, but we suffer losses as well. Soon the old front line is re-established but just we reach our assembly area the call goes out again, Panzers to the front. The Russians have launched another attack, the whole process seems continuous. The losses in Panzers and men are great.'*

## 10/11 AUGUST 1944

DURING THE NIGHT ELEMENTS OF *4. Kompanie* from *I./SS-Panzer-Regiment 3*, took up positions in Brzczowica. On the morning of the 11 August 1944, *4. Kompanie* suffered heavy Soviet anti-tank gunfire. This led to the loss of two Panthers which were hit on the eastern edge of Brzczowica by concealed Soviet anti-tank gunfire at the northern end of the village. The Panthers manage to destroy four Soviet anti-tank guns in counter fire.

On 11 August 1944, *SS-Hauptsturmführer* Zech took command of *SS-Panzer-Aufklärungs-Abteilung 3*.

On the same day elements of the *Stabskompanie* of *I./SS-Panzer-Regiment 3* were involved in a counterattack between Brzczowica and Solki providing support to *III./SS-Panzergrenadier-Regiment 5 'Totenkopf'*. In the late afternoon the Soviets tried to storm Kobylanka but the attack was pushed back the grenadiers of *III./SS-Panzergrenadier-Regiment 5 'Totenkopf'* and the Panthers from *I./SS-Panzer-Regiment 3*. During the evening, the *III./SS-Panzergrenadier-Regiment 5 'Totenkopf'* along with the attached Panthers had to fight a withdrawal battle to the division's front line; this was completed at 2200 hours.

Excerpt from the nomination report for the German Cross in Gold for *SS-Obersturmführer* von Kleist, *Chef* of 4. *Kompanie*:

*Defensive fighting north-east of Stanislawow on 11 August 1944*

*During the night of the 10/11 August 1944, the main line of resistance running from Kobylanka to Brzczowica was pulled back during the morning hours on 11 August 1944 after the Russians attacked the positions of* SS-Panzergrenadier-Regiment 5 'Totenkopf' *near Brzczowica with strong infantry and tank forces. Under the command of* SS-Obersturmführer *von Kleist, 4. Kompanie set out and counterattacked at the eastern edge of Brzczowica. Quickly driving into the attack, the* Kompanie *lost two Panthers as total losses from anti-tank gunfire, fired from the northern edge of the village. The* Kompanie *also took flanking fire from positions between the houses in Brzczowica. Another* Kompanie *from I./SS-Panzer-Regiment 3 attacked from the west. During the fighting 4. Kompanie destroyed three anti-tank guns after driving over them. Since there was no escorting infantry, the crews from 4. Kompanie were forced to defend themselves repeatedly with MPi and hand-held weapons. They fought amongst the houses of the village and repelled Russian tank destruction squads. Due to the rapid counterattack by* SS-Obersturmführer *von Kleist and his* Kompanie, *the Russians were forced to withdraw from Brzczowica and pull back to the south of the village. With energetic leadership and skilled use of his tanks,* SS-Obersturmführer *von Kleist was able to recapture Brzczowica after a short battle. Later a Russian counterattack with infantry and tanks was repulsed.*

## 12 AUGUST 1944

THE *I./SS-PANZER-REGIMENT 3* WAS INVOLVED in defensive actions in the area of Radzymin and Rembertow.

## 14 AUGUST 1944

ELEMENTS OF *I./SS-PANZER-REGIMENT 3* IN Rembertow came under Soviet artillery fire.

*SS-Oberscharführer* Steiger again reports:
*'Here we are reunited with the support elements. Our living quarters are holes dug underneath our Panzer; this is safe against the shell splinters. Our night-time quarters are located some distance from the front line; here we can chase lice, clean weapons, rest and refuel. During the day we get post and the clerk has to write letters back home to families who suffered losses. The maintenance group under Lochmann and Fleuter keep the Panzers and vehicles in working order. We spend the day under a blue sky. A remote Russian artillery battery fires two shells into our assembly area; this causes some slight confusion but soon enough the order arrives – Panzers to the front!'*

## 18 AUGUST 1944

ELEMENTS OF THE *PANTHER-ABTEILUNG* IN Radzymin and Rembertow were moved into the area of Wola-Roszczep.

*SS-Oberscharführer* Steiger reports:
*'Over in Radzymin our quarters have to be moved into the area of Wola-Roszczep.'*

During the day the Soviet 62nd Guards Heavy Tank Regiment equipped with JS-2 tanks took up positions in the woods east of Krusze. The Panthers engaged three JS-2s; the Soviets reported damaging three Panthers.

## 19 AUGUST 1944

THE *I./SS-PANZER-REGIMENT 3* ATTACKED AND broke through a Soviet anti-tank front in the area east of Wola-Roszczep with *1. Kompanie* in the lead causing the Soviets to withdraw. Meanwhile, the *Stabskompanie* were involved in an attack on Krusze.

*SS-Oberscharführer* Steiger again recalls:
*'The Panther of* SS-Oberscharführer *Baumeister is knocked out; fortunately the crew do not suffer any injuries'.*

Soviet forces were reported in the woods near Krusze. At 0400 hours the *I./SS-Panzer-Regiment 3* attacked the Soviet positions with seven Panthers of *1. Kompanie* at the point. During the attack a Panther was knocked out but the crew bailed out unscathed. The Panther of *SS-Obersturmführer* Schramm was badly shot up with hits to the tracks, gun mantle and barrel. The Panthers from *I./SS-Panzer-Regiment 3* launched counterattacks at 1100 and at 1140 hours and for most of the afternoon starting at 1340 hours. A JS-2 was knocked out by a Panther and another two JS-2s badly damaged. The Panthers continued their attack as Panzers from *SS-Panzer-Regiment 5* arrived to provide support near Kozly. The *IV. SS-Panzerkorps* reported that the day's action of the combined *Kampfgruppen* of *'Totenkopf'* and *'Wiking'* destroyed 21 soviet tanks and self-propelled guns. The *Tiger-Kompanie* was involved in a counterattack on Krusze. Three Tigers were lost by *9. Kompanie* during the afternoon.

## 20 AUGUST 1944

The *1. Kompanie* was in action in the wooded area around Krusze, repelling Soviet infantry attacks. The Panthers had no infantry support and relied on their on-board machine-gun fire and high explosive rounds for close-quarter protection. Ordnance officer *SS-Untersturmführer* Connert's Panther was sent by *SS-Sturmbannführer* Meierdrees to locate *1. Kompanie.* Connert successfully executed this task and remained with *1. Kompanie* for three days. A single *Panther-Kompanie* provided support to *I./SS-Panzergrenadier-Regiment 6 'Eicke'* in the woods west of Trojany. The *Panther-Kompanie* helped the battalion repel an attack by 400 Soviet riflemen accompanied by supporting tanks.

*SS-Oberscharführer* Steiger recalled:

*'The new day brings no clarification to the situation. We are surrounded. Our six Panthers are not in radio contact and we have no infantry support. We have a small amount of ammunition stored in the woods but soon the Russians begin their attack. Only with great difficulty do we ward them off. On the second night,* SS-Obersturmführer *Schramm orders the iron rations to be opened. Worse than the hunger is the agonising thirst.'*

For most of the day the Panthers of *I./SS-Panzer-Regiment 3* played cat and mouse with the JS-2s of the 62nd Heavy Guards Tank Regiment. The Panthers mounted roving patrols along the front line in an attempt to determine the firing positions of the 62nd Heavy Guards Tank Regiment.

## 21 AUGUST 1944

In the morning the Divisional Headquarters learned that a large Soviet attack on Koscielny was in progress after a heavy artillery barrage. This attack was conducted by a reinforced rifle battalion with tank support. The Panthers from *I./SS-Panzer-Regiment 3* were dispatched to assist the *III./SS-Panzergrenadier-*

*Regiment 6 'Eicke'*. After protracted defensive fighting, a new defensive line was established between Klembow and Trojany. A *Panther-Kompanie* from *I./SS-Panzer-Regiment 3* was still providing support to *I./SS-Panzergrenadier-Regiment 6 'Eicke'*. The Panthers again engaged Soviet forces in the woods west of Trojany. During the night the *I./SS-Panzergrenadier-Regiment 6 'Eicke'* took up new defensive positions near Klembow. In the woods near Krusze six Panthers from *1. Kompanie* were still playing cat and mouse with Soviet tanks and infantry.

## 22 AUGUST 1944

THE *1. KOMPANIE* LOCATED NEAR Krusze endured a night of Soviet artillery and mortar fire. Later the *Kompanie* was pulled back and placed into reserve. The bulk of the *Abteilung* was located in Wola-Rasztowska but *1. Kompanie* was in the wooded area near Krusze and was later involved in action near Trojany and Hill 94.

*SS-Oberscharführer* Steiger recounted:

*'We hear the sound of a tank engine...is this a Russian tank attack, no, it's one of own. It's the Panther of the ordnance officer,* SS-Untersturmführer *Connert.* SS-Sturmbannführer *Meierdrees had sent him to look for us. We follow him back to the* Abteilung *command post where, after 72 hours holed up in our Panzers, we can finally get out and stretch. During the fighting around Hill 94,* SS-Obersturmführer *Schramm received a head wound, leaving us thinking who would next lead the* Kompanie. *Also, Company Sergeant Major Guido Eck is busy bringing us rations... he drives around in a cross-country VW, sometimes dodging Russian artillery fire as he visits the combat sections.'*

## 23 AUGUST 1944

THE *I./SS-PANZER-REGIMENT 3* WAS SPREAD over the woods east of Zwierzyniec and Hill 94. Later parts of the *Abteilung* were involved in counterattacks near Wola-Rasztowska while other elements of the *Abteilung* were involved in a tank battle near Guzowattka which began soon after the Soviets bombard Guzowattka with heavy artillery fire – during which Hans Baumeister from *1. Kompanie* was killed by shell splinters – and lasted until 1500 hours. Under the command of *SS-Obersturmführer* von Kleist, *4. Kompanie* secured the withdrawal from Piecyska by forming a security line along the northern edge of the village where they came under Soviet anti-tank and artillery fire. The *4. Kompanie* returned fire knocking out two tanks, three self-propelled guns and four trucks. Another part of *4. Kompanie* set out to escort some motorised infantry in the direction of Wola-Ratztowska. The same Panthers led a local counterattack which reached the southern edge of Roszczep. *1. Kompanie* spent the night in Zwierzyniec on security duty during which they managed to knock out two Sherman tanks and was later recalled to the *Abteilung* command post.

Excerpt from the nomination report for the German Cross in Gold for *SS-Obersturmführer* von Kleist, *Chef* of *4. Kompanie:*

*Defensive fighting in the area northeast of Radzymin, 19 August 1944-24 August 1944.*

*On the afternoon of 23 August 1944,* I./SS-Panzer-Regiment 3 *moved from the area of Pieczyska and Radzymin. Under the leadership of* SS-Obersturmführer *von Kleist* 4. Kompanie *was assigned an area covering the flank north of Pieczyska which allowed our infantry to withdraw north-east along the Kraszw road. During the afternoon, the positions of* 4. Kompanie *came under strong Russian artillery fire and in the evening the Russians attacked with tanks and motorised infantry from Rosczep in the direction of Wola-Ratztowska with the objective of reaching the Radzymin-Wyskow highway.* SS-Obersturmführer *von Kleist with his* Kompanie *blocked the Russian advance during which* 4. Kompanie *destroyed two T-43* [probably T-34/85] *tanks, three SU-85 self-propelled guns and four trucks with mounted infantry. The remnants of this force pulled back to Rosczep, during which* 4. Kompanie *pursued the Russians and managed to reoccupy the old main line of resistance thereby preventing the capture of the main highway.*

**24 AUGUST 1944**

Elements of *I./SS-Panzer-Regiment 3* were involved in heavy defensive actions between Hill 96 and Hill 103 while *4. Kompanie* took up defensive positions in Rosczep.

**25 AUGUST 1944**

In the area of Lipinki *4. Kompanie* supported *SS-Panzergrenadier-Regiment 5 'Totenkopf'* with five Panthers. Some Panthers from *I./SS-Panzer-Regiment 3* were sent to assist *SS-Panzergrenadier-Regiment 9 'Germania'* at 0800 hours and helped repel a Soviet attack.

Excerpts from the nomination report for the German Cross in Gold for *SS-Obersturmführer* von Kleist, *Chef* of *4. Kompanie:*

*Defensive Fighting south-east of Radzymin, 25 August 1944-28 August 1944*

*On 25 August 1944,* SS-Obersturmführer *von Kleist, with five Panthers attached to* SS-Panzergrenadier-Regiment 5 'Totenkopf', *was in the area of Lipinki where the Russians, supported by tanks, were particularly strong. The* Kompanie *of* SS-Obersturmführer *von Kleist provided direct support to our infantry along this sector.*

*On 26 August 1944, the Russians attacked with infantry and pushed our main line of resistance further back to the west.* SS-Obersturmführer *von Kleist with his Panthers attacked towards the old main line of resistance while defending themselves against Russian infantry using MG, MPi and hand grenades. During the fighting two Panthers were rendered immobile and the crews had to bail out and defend their Panthers from Russian infantry who tried to capture the tanks intact. During the afternoon, our assault troops managed to retake the old main line of resistance.*

*On 27 August 1944, the Russians made repeated incursions into the open and wooded terrain. By the clever use of his three operational Panther tanks,* SS-Obersturmführer *von Kleist managed to knock out two Russian tanks while two of the Panthers in his force were immobilised.* SS-Obersturmführer *von Kleist was wounded during the action but remained with his* Kompanie *to lead his troops.*

*In the course of the 28 August 1944, the Russians attacked during the evening after their artillery barrage immobilized several Panthers which forced the crews to dismount and defend themselves against Russian infantry. The commander of the infantry support to* 4. Kompanie *was killed during the fighting after which* SS-Obersturmführer *von Kleist assumed command of the infantry group and successfully repelled all Russian attacks.* SS-Obersturmführer *von Kleist was badly wounded; this was his sixth wound.*

*Comments by Regimental Commander*

*He was the centre of the defence in the regimental sector; he led by his display of personal courage.*

*Signed, Laackmann*

## 25 AUGUST /26 AUGUST 1944

DURING THE NIGHT *SS-HAUPTSTURMFÜHRER* SÄUMENICHT was killed. *SS-Hauptsturmführer* Säumenicht had been transferred to *SS-Panzer-Regiment 5* on 5 May 1944.

Elements of *I./SS-Panzer-Regiment 3* defended the crossroads in Zawady.

## 26 AUGUST 1944

TWO PANTHERS FROM *4. KOMPANIE* suffered battle damage and needed repair after Soviet infantry tank-hunter teams tried to knock them out. On the same day, *SS-Sturmbannführer* Meierdrees requested the promotion of *SS-Obersturmführer* Lummitsch to *SS-Hauptsturmführer*. The request was endorsed by *SS-Obersturmbannführer* Laackmann, commander of *SS-Panzer-Regiment 3*, but was turned down by the divisional commander, *SS-Brigadeführer* Becker, because Lummitsch was only 24 years of age at the time.

## 26/27 AUGUST 1944

THE BULK OF THE *PANTHER-ABTEILUNG* was located in the area of Radzymin. The three Panthers attached to *5. SS-Panzer-Division 'Wiking'* returned on 1 September 1944. Two Panthers of *4. Kompanie* were immobilised by Soviet defensive fire and Soviet infantry tried to capture both crews but they defended their positions and pushed the Soviets back.

*SS-Oberscharführer* Steiger reported during this period:

*'We were attacking* [on 22 August] *along the main road from Warsaw to Bialystok when* SS-Obersturmführer *Schramm got a head wound but was still able to lead the* Kompanie. *During the same night we moved to secure the wooded area near the road junction for Radzymin-Wola. The next day* [on 23 August] *the Russians attacked with tanks* [three KV-1s and two Shermans] *which we managed to knock out at a range of 200 metres.* SS-Sturmbannführer *Meierdrees recalled us back to Radzymin to secure the rear sector for two days, but* [on 25 August] *after another tank alert we had to depart for the front line. The Russians had been preparing to assault Guzowattka. We reached the town around 1500 hours without seeing any Russian tanks; instead we were welcomed by strong artillery fire during which Hans Baumeister was killed by a splinter that passed through the hatch of the loader. We also learned during this period that* SS-Hauptsturmführer Säumenicht was killed during the night of the $25/26^{th}$ *August while serving with* SS-Panzer-Regiment 5. *The losses amongst the* Kompanien *were very high;* 2. Kompanie *only have five commanders left,* 3. Kompanie *has six, and* 4. Kompanie *have only three. The* Chef *of* 4. Kompanie, SS-Obersturmführer *Lummitsch was lightly wounded.* 1. Kompanie *has three commanders, Schramm, Lizjewski and Schäfer. For the next two days we secured the exit of Radzymin then we were called to assist 'Wiking' – the Russians had broken through their front lines. Our march was conducted at night* [on 29 August].'

### 27 AUGUST 1944

*4. Kompanie* managed to knock out three Soviet tanks but lost two Panthers from battle damage. *SS-Obersturmführer* von Kleist led a counterattack to rescue the trapped crews who managed to bail out. Both Panthers were sent for repair. Two men from *4. Kompanie* were wounded.

### 28 AUGUST 1944

The *I./SS-Panzer-Regiment 3* conducted security duty at the exit of Radzymin. During the day, the commander of *4. Kompanie, SS-Obersturmführer* von Kleist, was wounded for a sixth time. *SS-Obersturmführer* Herbatschek, commander of *3. Kompanie* temporarily took charge of *4. Kompanie* which then became part of *Kampfgruppe Herbatschek.*

### 29 AUGUST 1944

The *I./SS-Panzer-Regiment 3* was now located near Benjaminow, just to the south-east. An assembly of Soviet tanks was spotted in the woods near Morkre-

Nowe. Artillery from *SS-Panzer-Artillerie-Regiment 5* shelled the assembly area. Later, the Panthers from *I./SS-Panzer-Regiment 3* moved south from Benjaminow to engage the Soviet assembly area near Hill 98. Support for the Panthers was provided by *SS-Panzer-Aufklärungs-Abteilung 5* which was engaged in combat near Hill 87. Fighting alongside *SS-Panzer-Aufklärungs-Abteilung 5* were three Panthers from *I./SS-Panzer-Regiment 3* which supported *2.* and *3. Kompanien* in the area of Regentowka. The Soviet breakthrough attempt was stopped but the former front line could not be retaken. Later, *I./SS-Panzer-Regiment 3* withdrew to the east, towards Benjaminow.

Throughout July and August the loss of officers, platoon leaders and Panzer commanders had been immense: *2. Kompanie* had been reduced to five qualified tank commanders; *3. Kompanie* to six qualified tank commanders and *4. Kompanie* to just three qualified tank commanders. *SS-Obersturmführer* von Kleist was evacuated to hospital.

*SS-Oberscharführer* Steiger recounts:

*'As we assemble we come under a salvo of Russian rocket fire. Zeitler's Panther had to be returned to the* Werkstatt-Kompanie. *The* 1. Kompanie *has been split into two* Kampfgruppen*: one group is under the command of* SS-Obersturmführer *Schramm, the other under the command of* SS-Obersturmführer *Herbatschek. Herbatschek's* Gruppe *fought near Nadma.'*

**30 AUGUST 1944**

The *I./SS-Panzer-Regiment 3* saw intense combat in the area of Mokre, which was slightly east of Radzymin and along the main road from Radzymin to Zawady. In August 1944, the *I./SS-Panzer-Regiment 3* had only three combat officers left: Leciejewski, Schramm and Schäfer.

**31 AUGUST 1944**

Three Panthers from *1. Kompanie* attached to *II./SS-Panzer-Regiment 5* under the command of *SS-Hauptsturmführer* Flugel saw defensive action near Regentowka. The *1. Kompanie* had been split between two *Kampfgruppen* with three Panthers in each.

**1 SEPTEMBER 1944**

The *I./SS-Panzer-Regiment 3* and *5. Kompanie* of *II./SS-Panzer-Regiment 3* were in action in the area of Nadma and Slupno. After spending nearly a week as part of a separate *Kampfgruppe*, the tanks under the command of *SS-Obersturmführer* Schramm were regrouped and returned to the *Panther-Abteilung*. Meanwhile *1. Kompanie* defended the area of north of Nadma while *3. Kompanie* were situated near Slupno in support of *I./SS-Panzergrenadier-Regiment 5 'Totenkopf' (gepanzert)*. *SS-Obersturmführer* Lummitsch resumed command of *4. Kompanie* after recovering from the wound he sustained in late July.

## 2 SEPTEMBER 1944

Panthers from *3. Kompanie* of *I./SS-Panzer-Regiment 3* provided support to a battle group from the Hungarian 1st Cavalry Division during an attack on Nadma. *5. Kompanie* from *II./SS-Panzer-Regiment 3* was also on hand. Later, the Panthers and Panzer IVs were reinforced by Sturmgeschütze from *SS-Panzerjäger-Abteilung 3* which was fighting near Brzozowa, south-east of Nadma. The ordnance officer for *I./SS-Panzer-Regiment 3*, *SS-Untersturmführer* Steinegger, was wounded and replaced by *SS-Untersturmführer* Connert.

## 3 SEPTEMBER 1944

Five Panthers from *I./SS-Panzer-Regiment 3* were in the area of Benjaminow.

## 6 SEPTEMBER 1944

*1. Kompanie* assembled near Struga; the rest of the *Panther-Abteilung* was once more dispersed along the front line of the *'Totenkopf' Division*.

*SS-Oberscharführer* Steiger reported:

*'The* Kompanie *was recalled a week later by* SS-Obersturmbannführer *Laackmann. A forced march of 40km brought us near Serock on the Bug River. During the march the Panther of* SS-Unterscharführer *Köster caught fire due to a damaged fuel line and the tank was reduced to burnt-out wreck. At dawn we attacked the area where the Russians had broken through and by evening we had managed to straighten out the front line. The* Kompanie *managed to knock out several Russian tanks and we even managed to capture some Russian tractors. During the night we camped in a small wood.'*

## 7 SEPTEMBER 1944

Six Panthers from *1. Kompanie* of the *Panther-Abteilung* were sent to Serock from their assembly point near Struga to support *7. Kompanie* of the *SS-Panzer-Regiment 5* (with five operational Panthers) which was under the command of *SS-Untersturmführer* Olin. The Panthers of *SS-Panzer-Regiment 5* and *SS-Panzer-Regiment 3* were used to repel a Soviet attack which had broken through the *'Wiking'* divisional front line with 20 tanks. Three Panthers of *1. Kompanie* of *SS-Panzer-Regiment 3* were deployed north of Serock and another three west of Debinki. The *7. Kompanie* of the *SS-Panzer-Regiment 5* knocked out 11 Soviet tanks and captured two tanks.

*SS-Oberscharführer* Steiger recalled:

*'During the evening, the front line is straightened once more, our prime movers are captured by the Russians but we quickly recapture them.'*

**8 SEPTEMBER 1944**

The *Panther-Abteilung* was forced to withdraw 500 metres and formed a new line of resistance. *1. Kompanie* took up positions near Debinki with three Panthers while its other three Panthers were located just north-west of Serock.

**9 SEPTEMBER 1944**

*SS-Oberscharführer* Steiger recounts:

*'At 0400 hours we had to make ready for a march of 80km back to the gates of Warsaw. This time we moved south and rolled through Jablonna and finally reached Zabki during the late afternoon. We refuelled and took on provisions. Our supply trucks were barely out of sight when the Russian artillery came crashing down.* SS-Sturmbannführer *Meierdrees ordered our* Kompanie *to take up positions in the suburb of Praga, in Warsaw, to defend a road junction. We had received the strictest order not to retreat. The German front moved past us, troops flooded past our location with the Russians in pursuit but because of bad visibility we could only fire at the Russians at a short range. The heat was unbearable and inside the steel Panther it was torture. Later in the night a thunderstorm broke out. Using this as cover, the Russians tried to sneak some SU-85s past us but the first SU-85 was knocked out at 30 meters, the second one turned around and withdrew.'*

**10 SEPTEMBER 1944**

The *I./SS-Panzer-Regiment 3* was fighting defensively near Hill 104 and Slupno. To the west of Slupno the Soviets were trying to break through with tanks supported by strong artillery fire. The *I./SS-Panzergrenadier-Regiment 5 'Totenkopf' (gepanzert)* defended the area. From the woods near Pustelnik *5. Kompanie*, under the command of *SS-Untersturmführer* Tautkus, was ordered to make ready while the *2. Kompanie* of *SS-Panzerjäger-Abteilung 3* was committed 1km north of Hill 88. The *1. Kompanie* was ordered to leave Serock and re-assemble in the area of Praga as they returned to *I./SS-Panzer-Regiment 3*. The *Kompanie* had been put in reserve by the *IV. SS-Panzerkorps* near Zabki, 6km north-east of Praga. The *1. Kompanie* was then sent to provide support to the *73. Infanterie-Division*. After departing at 1100 hours it reported to the *73. Infanterie-Division* command post at 1130 hours.

Earlier that day, Soviets forces had breached the *73. Infanterie-Division* front lines, forcing it to relinquish Hill 106. The *1. Kompanie* arrived with 11 Panthers (later, six Panthers are reported operational). The *Kompanie* was attached to *Füsilier-*

*Bataillon 173* and saw action north-east of Zielona. At 1245 hours the Panthers were in the southern parts of Wawer and were joined by *1. Kompanie* (Hetzer) from *Panzerjäger-Abteilung 743*. At 1315 hours, the Panthers were north-west of Wawer, a single Panther having been immobilised by Soviet defensive fire. The *1. Kompanie* claimed two Soviet tanks. *1. Kompanie* was later moved to the area of Zabki to form the *IV. SS-Panzerkorps* reserve.

## 11 SEPTEMBER 1944

The *Panther-Abteilung* saw intensive combat in the area of Hill 104 and Slupno and was involved in a counterattack that morning which was brought to a halt by heavy Soviet anti-tank gunfire. Other elements of the *Panther-Abteilung* saw action in the area of Elsnerow and Wola-Radyminska. The *1. Kompanie* (with eight Panthers operational) along with *Füsilier-Bataillon 173* were in action in the area of a local brickyard. A prime mover from the *Berge-Zug* (rescue platoon) was knocked out near Wola. The *1. Kompanie* knocked out four Soviet tanks near Hill 96. On 10 and 11 September 1944, *1. Kompanie* knocked out a total of six Soviet tanks.

Later, Schramm was nominated for the *Ehrenblatt des Heeres* (German Army Roll of Honour Clasp) for his actions during 10/11 September 1944:

*Reasons given by Superior Officers:*

*On 10 and 11 September 1944, the* 1. Kompanie *under the command of* SS-Obersturmführer *Schramm was acting as Korps reserve in the area of Zabki, 6km north-east of Praga, Warsaw.*

*On 10 September 1944 and 11 September 1944, the enemy attacked in the direction of Rembertow with strong tank support.* Kampfgruppe *Schramm consisting of eight Panthers fought against the forward elements and knocked out six enemy tanks.*

*After the infantry had withdrawn and* Kampfgruppe *Schramm had lost one Panther as a total loss, the divisional commander of the* 73. Infanterie-Division *ordered* SS-Obersturmführer *Schramm to retake Zacisze and form a new security line.* SS-Obersturmführer *Schramm succeeded in his mission despite coming under heavy tank and anti-tank gunfire. He then deployed his operational Panthers (seven Pz. Vs) and formed a new security line under the most difficult of conditions.* SS-Obersturmführer *Schramm held steadfast in Zabki and prevented a breakthrough along the Korps' right flank and the rear areas of the* Panzer-Division 'Totenkopf' *and the Hungarian 1st Cavalry Division.*

*In the night between 12 and 13 September 1944, the enemy attacked with strong armoured forces against the northern part of Zabki and then Drewniza. On the morning of the 13 September 1944, after a strong artillery barrage, the enemy attacked again with tanks.* SS-Obersturmführer *Schramm, with energy and skilful use of his three Panthers, engaged in tank versus tank duels at close range and destroyed eight enemy tanks. The Panther of* SS-Obersturmführer *Schramm was hit rendering his main gun useless but he continued to lead his small* Panzergruppe *(two Pz. Vs) and destroyed another four enemy tanks which tried to attack the Praga-Radzymin highway. His small* Panzergruppe *continued to push the enemy back and prevented a breakthrough.*

SS-Obersturmführer *Schramm mastered often seemingly hopeless situations with great personal courage and managed to hold and break up repeated enemy tank assaults. The destruction of 28 enemy tanks by* Kampfgruppe Schramm *allowed the* IV. SS-Panzerkorps *to successfully redeploy and take up new positions.* SS-Obersturmführer *Schramm was killed on 19 September 1944.'*

*The Divisional Commander,* SS-Oberführer *Becker*

*Opinion of the Commanding General of the* IV. SS-Panzerkorps:
*This proposal is approved.*

SS-Gruppenführer and Generalleutant der Waffen-SS *Gille*

**12 SEPTEMBER 1944**

*1. Kompanie* was still attached to the *73. Infanterie-Division* defending Zabki and assigned to *Füsilier-Bataillon 173* and during the day claimed 16 Soviet tanks knocked out. Meanwhile *1. Kompanie* of *Panzerjäger-Abteilung 743* claimed a further three Soviet tanks knocked out. The *Panther-Abteilung* was spread over the following areas: Kaweczyn, Elsnerow and Zielonka.

Also during the day, *SS-Obersturmführer* Schramm launched a local counterattack with three Panthers and managed to establish a new defensive line at the eastern edge of Zacisze with the support of troops from the *73. Infanterie-Division.*

Other elements of *I./SS-Panzer-Regiment 3* continued their defensive actions around Hill 104. Also during the day *SS-Untersturmführer* Koleczek was wounded. This was reported to the *SS-FHA* on 13 September 1944 by the *'Totenkopf' Division.*

*SS-Oberscharführer* Steiger recounts:

*'At around 0300 hours we got a radio report telling us to return to Zabki. The Russians had broken through the front there and this threatened the flank. The demand for Panzers was constant but we had so few of them. The* I./SS-Panzer-Regiment 3 *was scattered across the front, fighting in small numbers and in various sectors, only*

SS-Sturmbannführer *Meierdrees knew the whole situation. We had to change radio frequencies every day because the Russians were sending us false orders and reports almost every day. During another local counterattack around Zabki, we encountered the latest model of the Josef Stalin tank; this was to cause us severe problems.'*

## 13 SEPTEMBER 1944

THE *1. KOMPANIE* WAS STILL defending the area of Zabki, along with *1. Kompanie* of *Panzerjäger-Abteilung 743*, *Füsilier-Bataillon 173* and elements of *Grenadier-Regiment 186*, and together they repelled several Soviet attacks. The Panther 122 (Ausf. G model) commanded by *SS-Unterscharführer* Köster was immobilised by Soviet anti-tank gunfire which also killed the driver, *SS-Rottenführer* Knopp. Due to the combat situation, the crew abandoned the vehicle. Later that night the crew, together with some scout troops, successfully recovered the Panther, before returning to the divisional front line during the early morning of the 14 September 1944. Panther 122 would eventually be lost during the afternoon of the 16 March 1945 south-east of Magyaralmás. The Soviets had tried to breach the front line with tanks during the day but the Panthers of *SS-Unterscharführer* Lommer and Reif knocked out eight of the Soviet tanks while under the command of *SS-Obersturmführer* Schramm. The *1. Kompanie* knocked out a total of 25 Soviet tanks. One Panther also provided covering fire for the *5. Kompanie* of *II./SS-Panzer-Regiment 3* during the fighting for Hill 104. Another single Panther provided security while covering the Praga-Radzymin road.

## 14 SEPTEMBER 1944

ELEMENTS OF *I./SS-PANZER-REGIMENT 3* ALONG with *5. Kompanie* of *II./SS-Panzer-Regiment 3* defended the area of Lewicpol while other elements of *I./SS-Panzer-Regiment 3* supported *2. Kompanie* from *SS-Panzer-Aufklärungs-Abteilung 3* during a counterattack on Kobylka.

## 15 SEPTEMBER 1944

FOR THE FIRST TIME, THE *I./SS-Panzer-Regiment 3* encountered the Soviet JS-1 heavy tank in the area of Zabki. Some Panthers were still providing support to *SS-Panzer-Aufklärungs-Abteilung 3* near Hill 104 while two Panthers were attached to *Grenadier-Regiment 186* near Lewicpol.

## 16 SEPTEMBER 1944

THE *PANTHER-ABTEILUNG* WAS INVOLVED IN defensive actions east of Rozopole and Hill 101. The Soviets managed to break through the defences of the Hungarian 1st Cavalry Division but counterattacks by elements of *I./SS-Panzer-Regiment 3* from the north and elements of the *19. Panzer-Division* from the south managed to close the gap in the area of Tomaszow. The fighting lasted nearly 24 hours. On the road north of Marki, a column of Soviet tanks from the 3rd Tank Corps were ambushed by Panthers from *I./SS-Panzer-Regiment 3*. The Soviets lost five T-34s and four US Sherman tanks during this engagement.

## 18 SEPTEMBER 1944

The *Panther-Abteilung* was still fighting defensive battles in the area of Rozopole, Hill 101 and Hill 103. The *I./SS-Panzer-Regiment 3* formed a new *Ausbildungs-Kompanie* for training the intake of *Luftwaffe* personnel transferred to the *Waffen-SS*. This *Kompanie* provided courses for platoon leaders and crews. During the fighting for Hill 101 and 103, four US Sherman tanks were captured by *5. Kompanie* of the *II./SS-Panzer-Regiment 3*.

*SS-Obersturmführer* Schramm was killed during the fighting near Tomaszow-Jablonna and Hill 101. Only the radio operator and the driver survive after the Panther is hit. *Kampfgruppe* Herbatschek was formed by the amalgamation of *1.* and *3. Kompanie* and *SS-Obersturmführer* Herbatschek assumed temporary command of *1. Kompanie*.

*SS-Oberscharführer* Martin Steiger reports:

*'The last* Kompanie *commander is dead* and we regret his loss. Schramm was an outstanding troop leader and he never carried out his duty due to ambition but with care and sacrifice. From Schramm's crew the gunner, loader, driver and radio operator were all seriously wounded. The day's battle rages all around Hill 101 and the Hill changes hands several times. The grenadiers take heavy losses; I was lightly wounded during the fighting and managed to stay with the support units. Upon recovery I was made a* Zugführer *in the training company and helped retrain ex-*Luftwaffe *personnel on the Panther tank. With the exception of a few short weeks the* II. Abteilung *has, since the spring of 1943, been involved in withdrawal battles all the way back into Romania. They, like us, suffer from personnel shortages.'*

*Note: Schramm's official date of death was cited as the 19 September 1944.

## 19 SEPTEMBER 1944

The *Panther-Abteilung* was in defensive action against Soviet attacks along the heights of Hills 96, 101, 103 and Tomaszow. In support of *I./SS-Panzer-Regiment 3* were *5.* and *6. Kompanie* (Panzer IVs) from *II./SS-Panzer-Regiment 3*.

## 20 SEPTEMBER 1944

The *I./SS-Panzer-Regiment 3* was involved in heavy combat for Hill 101 and Hill 96 in support of *I./SS-Panzergrenadier-Regiment 6 'Eicke'*. Tank support to the grenadiers was provided by *5. Kompanie* of the *II./SS-Panzer-Regiment 3.* The Panthers also provided cover for *16. Kompanie* of the *SS-Panzergrenadier-Regiment 6 'Eicke'.*

**21 SEPTEMBER 1944**

The *I./SS-Panzer-Regiment 3* was situated in the area of Hill 101 and the *Panther-Abteilung* came under heavy Soviet artillery fire. The *1. Kompanie*, now under the command of *SS-Hauptsturmführer* Balzer, was integrated with *2. Kompanie* to form *Kampfgruppe Balzer*. *SS-Obersturmführer* Herbatschek returned to *3. Kompanie.*

**22 SEPTEMBER 1944**

The *Stabskompanie* of the *I./SS-Panzer-Regiment 3* ended a two-day long attachment to *SS-Panzergrenadier-Regiment 6 'Eicke'* after taking part in the defensive fighting around Hill 97 and Hill 101.

**25 SEPTEMBER 1944**

The *I./SS-Panzer-Regiment 3* remained in the sector of Hill 101 and Rozopole.

**1 OCTOBER 1944**

The *I./SS-Panzer-Regiment 3* was involved in combat in the area of Hill 101. During the first week of October, *the Panther-Abteilung* was busy supporting *SS-Panzergrenadier-Regiment 5 'Totenkopf'* and *SS-Panzergrenadier-Regiment 6 'Eicke'.* On the same day, *SS-Untersturmführer* Werner Mittag was posted to the *SS-Pionier-Ausbildungs- und Ersatz-Regiment* in Dresden.

Excerpt from the evaluation report of *SS-Untersturmführer* Friedrich Mink dated 5 October 1944:

SS-Untersturmführer *Friedrich Mink*
*SS-Nr.: 19126*
Zugführer*: 1 March 1944*
*Married: 9 July 1932*
*Number of Children: 4*

1. *Personal Assessment:*
   *In character he is open and honest.*

2. *Mental and Physical state, Knowledge of Duties:*
   *In general he has an average mental and physical disposition. His knowledge of duties and are of a good average standard.*

3. *Behaviour and Attitude to Superiors, Comrades and Subordinates and off-duty Behaviour:*
   *His conduct and behaviour towards his superiors is soldierly, correct and proper. He is a favourite of his comrades. To his subordinates he is firm and strict but sometimes his judgement could be clearer and more defined. His off-duty behaviour is impeccable.*

4. *Ideological Orientations:*
   *Has a positive philosophical attitude but has less interest in lectures*

5. *Conduct before the Enemy and Specialist Tasks:*
   *He is a proven officer before the enemy and at the present he fills the post of* Zugführer *of the* Panzer-Pionierzug.

6. *Suitability for promotion:* (This section was left blank)

7. *Judgement and evaluation:* (This section was left blank)

8. *Main Comments:*
   *As leader of the* Panzer-Pionierzug *his service has been completed to my satisfaction but further course work must be considered as this will allow him to be more determined against the enemy.*

*Signed,* SS-Sturmbannführer and Abteilungsführer
*Meierdrees*

*Additional Comments:*
*In agreement with the above.*

*Signed,* SS-Obersturmbannführer and Regimentsführer
*Laackmann*

Excerpt from the evaluation report on *SS-Untersturmführer* Gerhard Koleczek, dated 5 October 1944:

SS-Untersturmführer *Gerhard Koleczek*
*SS-Nr.: 476259*
Zugführer: *1 March 1944*
*Married: N/A*
*Number of Children: N/A*

1. *Personal Assessment:*
   *Koleczek does not appear to have much of an outward-going personality; in character he is very quiet which makes it very difficult to get a true sense of his character.*

2. *Mental and Physical State, Knowledge of Duties:*
   *In terms of his mental and physical state, including his knowledge of his expected duty, he is average.*

3. *Attitude to Superiors, Comrades and Subordinates and Off-duty Behaviour:*
   *His behaviour towards his superiors and subordinates is good. His off duty behaviour is correct.*

4. *Ideological Orientations:*
   *Ideologically he is correct but he does try to be more convincing.*

5. *Conduct before the Enemy and Specialist Tasks:*
   *He is proven before the enemy and currently fills the post of* Zugführer *in a* Panzer-Kompanie.

6. *Suitability for Promotion:*
   *At this time suitability cannot be determined as Koleczek is recovering from a wound.*

7. *Judgement and Evaluation:* (This section was left blank)

8. *Main Comments:*
   *Koleczek needs more training courses as an SS-Officer in the Panzer Troops in order to retain his post as* Zugführer.

*Signed,* SS-Sturmbannführer and Abteilungsführer
*Meierdrees*

*Additional Comments:*
*In agreement with the above.*

*Signed,* SS-Obersturmbannführer and Regimentsführer
*Laackmann*

Excerpt from the evaluation report on *SS-Obersturmführer* Alfred Quilitz dated 5 October 1944:

SS-Obersturmführer der Reserve *Alfred Quilitz*
*SS-Nr.: 54681*
Abteilungs-Nachrichten-Zugführer*: 21 June 1944*

1. *Personal Assessment:*
   *Quilitz has held the post of* Abteilungs-Nachrichten-Zugführer *since 6 November 1942. In character he is quiet and unassuming but he has served in the current position with total satisfaction.*

2. *Mental, Physical state and Knowledge of Duties:*
   *His disposition regarding his mental and physical state is average; knowledge of his duties is average.*

3. *Behaviour and Attitude towards Superiors, Subordinates and Comrades:*
   *His behaviour towards his superiors is correct and soldierly. Towards his comrades and subordinates, Quilitz is very popular but he must be stricter and in time this will come.*

4. *Ideological Orientations:*
   *Quilitz has a 'consolidated ideology' but he must take the matter more seriously and be persuaded during lectures so he can be more freely convinced.*

5. *Conduct before the Enemy and Specialist Tasks:*
   *As Signals Officer for the Abteilung he has kept the communications of the Abteilung working and in place despite enemy efforts. He served in his current role correctly.*

6. *Suitability for Promotion:*
   *At the current time Quilitz could not be promoted due to illness.*

7. *Judgement and Evaluation:*
   *As* Nachrichten-Zugführer *for the* Abteilung *he shows good tactical awareness when carrying out his combat duties. He has contributed to the success of the* Abteilung.

8. *Additional Comments:*
   *(Left blank).*

*Signed,* SS-Sturmbannführer und Abteilungsführer
*Meierdrees*

## 10 OCTOBER 1944

*4. Kompanie* WAS INVOLVED IN very heavy fighting for Hills 103 and 105. The rest of *I./SS-Panzer-Regiment 3* was deployed between the heights 101 and 103 in support of *I./SS-Panzergrenadier-Regiment 6 'Eicke'*. Again the *Panther-Abteilung* came under severe Soviet artillery fire. The supply units for the *Kompanien* were located in Palmyrj, near Modlin.

*SS-Oberscharführer* Gumbl was badly wounded when Panther 431 was hit and Panther 122 was hit yet again, this time killing *SS-Unterscharführer* Köster. *SS-Untersturmführer* Müller was posted into the *1. Kompanie*. At this time, *1. Kompanie* was providing direct support to *I./SS-Panzergrenadier-Regiment 6 'Eicke'*. At the command post of *III./SS-Panzergrenadier-Regiment 5 'Totenkopf'*, a Panther from the *Stabskompanie I./SS-Panzer-Regiment 3* along with two self-propelled 2cm *Flak-Vierling* guns arrived and waited for an artillery observer SPW from *IV. (schwere)/SS-Panzer-Artillerie-Regiment 3* to conduct a mission in the sector of *SS-Panzergrenadier-Regiment 10 'Westland'*. The Panther had come from Michalow.

*SS-Oberscharführer* Steiger reports:

*'During the day one of our Panthers* [*SS-Unterscharführer* Köster's tank] *is struck by a Russian artillery shell.'*

*SS-Sturmbannführer* Meierdrees wrote the following concerning *SS-Obersturmführer* Quilitz's actions from the 10 October 1944:

*'As the signals officer for the* Abteilung *for the last two years,* SS-Obersturmführer *Quilitz has distinguished himself with determination and bravery, especially during the recent fighting for Hill 97 on 10 October 1944. During heavy close-quarter fighting near the enemy's positions, the Panther of* SS-Obersturmführer *Quilitz suffered track damage. Without regard to his personal safety he dismounted and quickly carried out emergency repairs to the track thus allowing the Panther to return to the fight against the enemy.'*

## 11 OCTOBER 1944

*SS-Sturmbannführer* BIERMEIER, COMMANDING OFFICER OF *II./SS-Panzer-Regiment 3* visited the command post of *2. Kompanie/ SS-Panzer-Pionier-Bataillon 3*. During a Soviet artillery barrage the command post took a direct hit and Biermeier was seriously wounded. Meanwhile, the Panthers from *I./SS-Panzer-Regiment 3* defended Hill 97 and supported the grenadiers from *II./SS-Panzergrenadier-Regiment 6 'Eicke'* and at least one counterattack was mounted, along with the Panthers from the *Stabskompanie*.

## 12 OCTOBER 1944

The *Panther-Abteilung* was involved in heavy defending near Rozopole. The divisional artillery from the *19. Panzer-Division* provided fire support in sector of the *3. SS-Panzer-Division 'Totenkopf'*.

## 13 OCTOBER 1944

The *I./SS-Panzer-Regiment 3* was in the area of Michalow, providing flank protection for the *3. SS-Panzer-Division 'Totenkopf'*.

## 14 OCTOBER 1944

The *I./SS-Panzer-Regiment 3* was still located in the area of Rozopole. *SS-Obersturmführer* Schramm was recommended for the award of the *Ehrenblatt des Heeres* for his defensive actions during mid-September 1944.

## 15 OCTOBER 1944

Elements of *I./SS-Panzer-Regiment 3* were in action in the area of Josefow and Hill 97. During the day the *Panther-Abteilung* managed to repel an attack by Soviet tanks with the assistance of *9. Kompanie* (Tiger) from *SS-Panzer-Regiment 3*. The Tigers knocked out three Soviet tanks and the Panthers claimed another three.

## 17 OCTOBER 1944

Elements of the *Panther-Abteilung* were engaged in defensive actions in the area of Josefow.

## 22 OCTOBER 1944

The *Panther-Abteilung* was situated in Jablonna-Legionowo.

## 25 OCTOBER 1944

*SS-Obersturmführer* von Kleist was nominated for the German Cross in Gold.

## 27 OCTOBER 1944

The *I./SS-Panzer-Regiment 3*, along with the rest of *SS-Panzer-Regiment 3*, withdrew from its positions to reassemble behind the Brodnowski Canal, near the outflow of the Narew River, just north of Lajsk.

## 28 OCTOBER 1944

*SS-Obersturmführer der Reserve* Quilitz was awarded the Iron Cross First Class.

## 31 OCTOBER 1944

The *I./SS-Panzer-Regiment 3* counterattacked a limited Soviet advance along the railway track connecting Jablonna-Legionowo to Modlin. *SS-Untersturmführer* Leciejewski was wounded and, after recovering from his wounds, was posted to the *SS-Panzer-Ausbildungs- und Ersatz-Regiment.*

## 1 NOVEMBER 1944

The *I./SS-Panzer-Regiment 3* was based in Jablonna-Legionowo and Szybalin came under heavy Soviet artillery fire. Meanwhile, *1. Kompanie* enjoyed a rather quiet day; the *Kompanie-Spiess, SS-Hauptscharführer* Eck, travelled to Palmiry to collect rations and the crews found time for some much needed sleep.

*SS-Oberscharführer* Steiger reported:

*'In the Vistula bend things are quiet. The grenadiers dig themselves in. After taking up tank positions the crew can finally get some real rest and sleep. Our* Kompanie-Spiess, *Guido Eck, is in Palmiry gathering rations. Because of the current situation the quality of the food has improved.'*

Of the Panthers in the *Stabskompanie*, only four remained from the July 1944 issue, the turret numbers were as follows: Befehlspanther I01 and Befehlspanther I02 from the *Panzer-Aufklärungszug*, and Panthers I03 and I05.

## 5 NOVEMBER 1944

The *Armeeoberkommando 9* informed the *3. SS-Panzer-Division 'Totenkopf'* to order the *I./SS-Panzer-Regiment 3* and two battalions from *SS-Panzergrenadier-Regiment 5 'Totenkopf'* into the area south-east of Modlin as the *Armee* reserve.

On the same day *SS-Untersturmführer* Koleczek was transferred from the 1st Reserve Hospital in Posen to the *SS-Panzer-Ausbildungs- und Ersatz-Regiment* at Bitsch.

## 6 NOVEMBER 1944

The *I./SS-Panzer-Regiment 3*, moved into the area of Lomna-Niemicki as part of the *Armeeoberkommando 9* reserve. The rest of *SS-Panzer-Regiment 3* (minus *8. Kompanie*) was also in the area of Lomna-Niemicki.

*SS-Unterscharführer* Söhrmann (*Stabskompanie* of *I./SS-Panzer-Regiment 3*) reported:

*'We move back into the area of Bug River's firth and finally we can look forward to some decent rest. During the recent battles the crews have finally merged together but we are also joined by some new personnel transferred from the* Luftwaffe.*'*

**9 NOVEMBER 1944**

Two new Bergepanthers arrived and were handed over to the *Werkstatt-Kompanie* of *SS-Panzer-Regiment 3* along with a Bergepanther from the *Panzer-Werkstattzug* of *I./SS-Panzer-Regiment 3* in Legionowo. One of the new Bergepanthers was a rebuilt Ausf. A model with a *Zimmerit* paste overlay. Both Bergepanthers were painted in factory yellow. The *Panzer-Werkstattzug* for the *Panther-Abteilung* only had one Bergepanther remaining on hand and several 18-ton prime mover towing vehicles. During November new recruits were assigned to the *Bergepanther-Zug* where they were given training on the correct use of tow cables and the other recovery equipment. With the increasing scarcity of fuel, the *Berge-Zug* was forced to use *Panjewagen* (horse drawn peasant wagons) to transport its supplies.

**12 NOVEMBER 1944**

At this point in time the *I./SS-Panzer-Regiment 3* with 14 Panthers was still attached to *SS-Panzergrenadier-Regiment 5 'Totenkopf'* and positioned south of Modlin. Both units were still acting as *Armeeoberkommando 9* reserve.

**15 NOVEMBER 1944**

*SS-Oberscharführer* Steiger wrote that the graves of Schramm, Biermeier and *SS-Unterscharführer* Köster were to be found in the military cemetery in Modlin.

**17 NOVEMBER 1944**

Befehlspanther I01 received technical maintenance in Bugmunde (Nowy-Dwor) by the repair section for *I./SS-Panzer-Regiment 3* and *Obersturmführer* Schramm was posthumously awarded the *Ehrenblatt des Heeres*.

**24 NOVEMBER 1944**

Two new Bergepanthers were delivered and issued to the *Werkstatt-Kompanie* of *SS-Panzer-Regiment 3*. On the same day, *SS-Obersturmführer* Quilitz was awarded the Panzer Assault Badge in Silver.

**26 NOVEMBER 1944**

*SS-Panzer-Regiment 3* was assembled and quartered in Neustadt.

**27 NOVEMBER 1944**

*SS-Untersturmführer* Köster was released from hospital and transferred to the *SS-Panzer-Ausbildungs- und Ersatz-Regiment*.

**29 NOVEMBER 1944**

NEAR THE BUG RIVER MOUTH, the *Werkstatt-Zug* carried out overdue repairs. The rest of November 1944 was spent quietly.

Throughout most of November 1944, the Panthers and motorised vehicles were given a thorough maintenance overall and all weapons were cleaned. Also, many of the personnel had to perform two-hour shifts at the *Abteilung*'s vehicle park carrying out various duties. *SS-Obersturmführer* Oeynhausen was transferred to the *Stabskompanie* of *SS-Panzer-Regiment 3* and made *Adjutant* for the regiment.

**1 DECEMBER 1944**

*SS-OBERSTURMFÜHRER* VON KLEIST AND *SS-UNTERSTURMFÜHRER* Leciejewski were both posted to the *SS-Panzer-Ausbildungs- und Ersatz-Regiment* in Sennelager.

**2 DECEMBER 1944**

THE *PANTHER-ABTEILUNG* MOVED FROM LOMNA-NIEMICKI to the area of Modlin. During December, many wounded personnel who had recovered returned to the *Panther-Abteilung*. The *I./SS-Panzer-Regiment 3* again conducted a march into a new assembly area, this time into the area of Okunin. The *Werkstatt-Zug* was quartered in Nowo-Miastro.

*SS-Rottenführer* Lindenau from *3. Kompanie* reported:

*'Our* Kompanie *is led by* SS-Obersturmführer *Herbatschek. Panther 333 is under the command of* SS-Unterscharführer *Sutter.* SS-Unterscharführer *Picha was killed some time back. I'm still the gunner.* SS-Rottenführer *Wendland is the driver and our Jupp Hille is still the radio operator.'*

**5 DECEMBER 1944**

*SS-UNTERSCHARFÜHRER* SÖHRMANN RECALLED THAT DURING every move, the *Stabskompanie* had to take every item with it, including furniture.

**15 DECEMBER 1944**

*SS-OBERSTURMFÜHRER DER RESERVE* LINSENMAYER WAS posted from *SS-Panzer-Ausbildungs- und Ersatz-Regiment* to *I./SS-Panzer-Regiment 3* as a *Kompanie-Chef.* Upon arrival he took command of *2. Kompanie*. Linsenmayer had originally served with the '*Leibstandarte*' from 1936 to 1940. From September 1940 to January 1942 he spent time at the *SS-Kradschützen-Ersatz-Bataillon* in Ellwangen. Later, he was posted to the *6. SS-Gebirgs-Division 'Nord'*. On 15 March 1943 he was transferred to the new *10. SS-Panzergrenadier-Division 'Frundsberg'* and arrived on 16 March 1943. In January 1944 he was posted to the *Panther-Abteilung* of

*SS-Panzer-Regiment 10* and took part in a *Kompanieführer-Lehrgang* at Versailles between 3 January 1944 and 29 January 1944. On 28 June 1944 he was made a *Kompanie-Chef* and remained as such until 20 November 1944 when he was transferred back to the *SS-Panzer-Ausbildungs- und Ersatz-Regiment.* On 15 December 1944 he was posted to *I./SS-Panzer-Regiment 3* where upon his arrival, *Kampfgruppe Balzer* was disbanded with *SS-Hauptsturmführer* Balzer resuming command of *1. Kompanie.*

**18 DECEMBER 1944**

The former *IVa* of the *Panther-Abteilung, SS-Untersturmführer* Wolf, was reported KIA (killed in action) while serving with the *21. Waffen-Gebirgs-Division der SS 'Skanderbeg'.*

**24 DECEMBER 1944**

Orders were issued for departure and rail transport to Hungary. The loading of 27 Panthers took place in the railway station of Nasielsk near Modlin while two other Panthers still requiring long-term repair were left with *SS-Panzer-Instandsetzungs-Abteilung 3.* The transports left on 26 December 1944.

**28 DECEMBER 1944**

After unloading in Raab (Győr), the Panthers were given a whitewash coating as winter camouflage. During the night of 28/29 December 1944, the last transport arrived carrying the *Werkstatt-Zug.*

**31 DECEMBER 1944**

*SS-Unterscharführer* Söhrmann recalled:

*'Spirits are running high, it's New Years Eve. The alcohol flows freely; our motto is, enjoy the war because the peace will be hell. The entire headquarters company is gathered – from the* Abteilung *commander down to the last man. At midnight we go outside to look at the night sky – it seems to have a reddish hue.'*

# CHAPTER 3

★ ★ ★

I./SS-Panzer-Regiment 3 in 1945

## 3.1. Combat in Hungary, 1 January 1945 - 15 March 1945

### Overview

On 29 October 1944, Soviet and Romanian forces launched an offensive to capture the capital of Hungary, Budapest. In the opening phase of the operation the Soviet forces overran huge areas of territory. By 26 December 1944 the Soviets had reached the Danube River and were attacking Budapest from both the north and the south, encircling around 70,000 German and Hungarian soldiers inside the capital. The German response was to launch a series of relief operations between 1 January 1945 and 26 January 1945 under the codenames 'Konrad', 'Konrad 2' and 'Konrad 3'. Within this framework the IV. SS-Panzerkorps with the *3. SS-Panzer-Division 'Totenkopf'* and the *5. SS-Panzer-Division 'Wiking'* were transferred from Poland to Hungary in late December 1944. The *3. SS-Panzer-Division 'Totenkopf'* took part in operations 'Konrad' and 'Konrad 2'.

### 1 JANUARY 1945

The *Panther-Abteilung* remained in Raab (Győr) and formed a scout platoon consisting of three Panthers in readiness for the upcoming operation.

*SS-Oberscharführer* Steiger recalls January 1945 as follows:

*'At Christmas we got an alert order – the division was to relocate to Hungary. Loading took place between Christmas and New Year's Day at Nasjelske near Modlin. Two days later we unloaded in Raab (Győr). The* Abteilung *made ready for the new attack. The assembly took place on both sides of the Danube River. The mission was to advance between Tata and the Danube and then join up in the wooded terrain on the northern slopes of the Vértes hills between Bicske and Zsámbék. That was the first objective; the second objective was then to advance on Budapest. The attack began*

*on 1 January 1945 at 1800 hours, without artillery fire. The roads through the hills were heavily mined by the Russians and they had also constructed heavy anti-tank barriers which blocked certain roads. Despite these obstacles the first objectives were quickly reached. On 4 January 1945* [2 January 1945 actually] SS-Sturmbannführer *Meierdrees was killed in Dunaalmás. The commander's Panzer took a direct hit in the turret. His body was later taken to Vienna for burial where he was laid next to Novotny, the heroic pilot. We reached the line Bicske-Zsámbék on 5 January but the Russian defensive front was getting stronger and soon began counterattacking. The defensive fighting lasted until 6 January.'*

*SS-Unterscharführer* Söhrmann recalled:

*'We wake up at the crack of dawn and have a hangover; breakfast is cooked in gourmet style. Afterwards we coat our tanks white with chalk. Maintenance on the tracks is a filthy business but all the fresh air and working outdoors does us good. We are informed that the battle will begin early on 2 January.'*

## 2 JANUARY 1945

At 0600 hours, after a final briefing, the Panthers and the other Panzers from *SS-Panzer-Regiment 3* move from the assembly area to begin their advance from Komárom along the road following the bank of the River Danube towards Szőny. A scout group of three Panthers moved at speed, the Tigers from *9. (schwere) Kompanie* were in the lead, next came the three Panthers with two Bergepanthers following on at 30 metres distance.

The *Panther-Abteilung* moved at slow speed. Elements of the *3. SS-Panzer-Division 'Totenkopf'* reached the western edge of Dunaalmás where they were involved in heavy fighting. As the Tigers and Panthers entered Dunaalmás, the lead Tiger was immobilized by Soviet defensive fire. *SS-Sturmbannführer* Meierdrees, in Panther I01, drove past the stricken Tiger to take the lead. Behind *SS-Sturmbannführer* Meierdrees was *Adjutant SS-Obersturmführer* Strobl in Panther I02. Meierdrees ordered a halt.

At 0645 hours, Meierdrees ordered the resumption of the advance. As *SS-Sturmbannführer* Meierdrees' Panther moved forward, a concealed SU-85 self-propelled gun from the 1,438th Self-Propelled Artillery Regiment, attached to the 170th Tank Brigade (18th Tank Corps), fired a round into the bottom-rear of the turret of Panther I01. The detonation blew the turret clear of the hull, killing Meierdrees and the turret crew (loader *SS-Sturmmann* Sepp Tittel and gunner *SS-Obersturmführer* Quilitz). The Panther rolled off the road and smashed into a house just to the right of the main road. The driver (*SS-Unterscharführer* Sepp Hirsch) and radio operator (*SS-Unterscharführer* Kurt Söhrmann) survived.

Panther I03 from the *Stabskompanie* fired one round into the SU-85 self-propelled gun, setting the vehicle on fire. Panther I01 was later recovered by a Bergepanther, call sign Bw I (*Berge-Wanne I*) from the *Werkstatt-Zug* of the *I./ SS-Panzer-Regiment 3*. During the recovery process a concealed Soviet 90mm anti-tank gun – a US lend-lease weapon – fired four rounds at the Bergepanther but all four rounds missed their target. Panther I01 was towed to Ács for repairs under the supervision of *SS-Unterscharführer* Hirsch.

The bodies of Quilitz and Tittel were taken to Komárom while the body of *SS-Sturmbannführer* Meierdrees was transported to Vienna. *SS-Obersturmführer der Reserve* Quilitz was laid to rest in the cemetery of Tata-Tóváros.

The command of the *Panther-Abteilung* was now taken over by *SS-Obersturmführer* Lummitsch. *SS-Scharführer* Jensen assumed temporary command of *4. Kompanie* (*SS-Scharführer* Jensen had been serving as the *Kompanie-Spiess* at the time).

As the Panthers continued their advance on Neszmély from the east, they encountered a Soviet motorised column. The Panthers fired on the trucks and crushed the anti-tank guns in the column under their tracks. By 0900 hours, the Panthers had advanced onto the heights south of Karva and, at around midday, they approached Nyergesújfalu. As they entered the western edge of the village, they were involved in a tank-versus-tank duel. At around 0100 hours on 3 January 1945, the *Panther-Abteilung* pushed towards Bajót but the Panther scout platoon discovered that the road had been blocked with anti-tank mines.

*SS-Rottenführer* Lindenau of *3 Kompanie* recalled:

*'At 0600 hours our Panthers begin the advance through the village of Füzítőpuszta and along the Danube River. On the right of the battalion Bachmann* [II./SS-Panzergrenadier-Regiment 5 'Totenkopf'] *scours the area.'*

*SS-Unterscharführer* Söhrmann recalled:

*'We awoke early. Sepp Hirsch lets the engine idle until it's warm. I connect the radios to regimental and the* Abteilung *radio network. Our loader is* SS-Sturmmann *Tittel and our second radio operator is* SS-Obersturmführer *Quilitz. He keeps in contact with the companies and the platoons.* SS-Obersturmführer *Quilitz is also the gunner; of course the last place belongs to the commander. Over the intercom we can hear his voice clearly, he asks if everything is in order and we all reply: "Jawohl* Sturmbannführer"*. The commander tells Sepp: "let's go! The Tigers will lead."'*

*SS-Unterscharführer* Söhrmann continued:

*'The Tigers fall out, one after the other.* SS-Sturmbannführer *Meierdrees is now in the lead. Behind us is* SS-Obersturmführer *Strobl, our* Adjutant. *It's still dark and so far no*

*one has shot at us yet. Suddenly* SS-Sturmbannführer *Meierdrees stops and dismounts, after some time we began to ask what is going on.* SS-Obersturmführer *Quilitz explains that the commander wanted to discuss the course of action once the battle begins.'*

*SS-Unterscharführer* Söhrmann recounts what happened in Dunaalmás:

*'The commander looked down at his watch and said: "Sepp, let's go". It was 0645 hours. All of a sudden a terrible, loud explosion occurs in the fighting compartment and there is a bright flash of red light and intense heat. The turret has been hit. Somehow Sepp and I manage to bail out of the Panther and fall onto the road. Sepp tries to remount the Panther but the tank just continues to roll forward. The turret crew are all dead.'*

One crew member from the Bergepanther sent to recover Panther I01 recalled the aftermath of this incident:

*'We were about 100 metres behind the lead Panzers when Meierdrees' tank was hit. We were ordered to recover the stricken Panther. As we hooked up the tow cables to the Panther, the Russians were firing a US lend-lease 9cm anti-tank gun at us. They tried to hit us four times but all the shots went wide and struck the house that Meierdrees' Panther had hit after rolling off the road.'*

*SS-Unterscharführer* Söhrmann also reported:

'SS-Sturmbannführer *Meierdrees was lifted out of the turret. Also killed were* SS-Obersturmführer *Quilitz and* SS-Sturmmann *Tittel. Sepp and I stand and look down at our highly esteemed commander and weep.'*

*SS-Rottenführer* Lindenau of *3 Kompanie* reported that elsewhere:

*'The local population welcomes us. Many of the women report that the Russians have raped them. A lot of Hungarians want to join us and try to jump on our Panthers – they also want to get weapons so they can fight and kill Russians; they are full of hate.'*

Franz Gschwandtner recalled*:*

*'On the morning of the 2 January we advanced along the Donau road. We lost the* Befehlspanzer (command tank) *I01 of* SS-Sturmbannführer *Meierdrees. During the recovery process the Russians tried to knock out our* Bergepanthers *with four shots from a concealed ambush position – all four shots missed us. It was common practice to have a* Bergepanthers *as close as possible to the lead Panthers during a combat operation.'*

## 3 JANUARY 1945

As the *Panther-Abteilung* advanced along the Nyergesújfalu-Bajót road it came under Soviet air attack from Il-2 aircraft of the 10th Assault Air Corps (17th Air Army). The advance on Bajót was led by *SS-Obersturmführer* Herbatschek of

*3. Kompanie*, along a road through woods. During the day Bajót was seized and the Panthers then prepared to advance on Bajna.

During the advance on Bajna, *I./SS-Panzer-Regiment 3* stopped to take on fuel and ammunition. As they neared Bajna, two Panthers turned off the road and drove into the open terrain in order to flank the village and attack a Soviet anti-tank strongpoint. In Bajna the Panthers again engaged Soviet tank forces. During the fighting for Bajna, the lead platoon consisting of three Tigers, with the Panthers following on, advanced slowly along the high street. Near the village church, a Soviet tank was knocked out. As the three Tigers approached the church, the lead Tiger was immobilized. The second Tiger drove past the stricken Tiger but was immobilized by 85mm tank rounds that hit its running gear. The third Tiger and a single Panther provided covering fire for the two damaged Tigers. The commander of the *Tiger-Kompanie* requested air support from the *Luftwaffe*. About 10 minutes later two JU-88 bombers[1] flew over.

During the fighting for Bajna *SS-Rottenführer* Lindenau of *3 Kompanie* reported:

'The Russians try to cross us out with bombs which hit ground right next to our tank 301. They only cause minor injuries. At one moment, the Soviet pilots turn around and flee in terror, dropping their bombs without any targeting in the area. We discover German fighters in the air; we are relieved.

However, instead of going after the Soviet bombers, they descend upon us and "rake" us with their on-board weapons. We are quick to throw orange tracer smoke...'

*SS-Rottenführer* Lindenau recalled that later:

*'SS-Obersturmführer Herbatschek was replaced by me in the commander's cupola. Suddenly I had a low-hanging overhead telephone cable wrapped around my neck. I was not able to get my arm and hand free but the cable was still around my neck. I tried shouting at the tank to stop. I'm thinking is this how I will die – hanged by telephone cable! I can see the cable beginning to stretch across the road, fortunately the cable, the one that's wrapped around my neck, snapped against the cupola'*

## 4 JANUARY 1945

DURING THE DAY, THE *PANTHER-ABTEILUNG* advanced along the road from Bajna to Szomor. Again during the march the Panthers had to battle Soviet tanks and anti-tank gunfire. The advance guard of the *Panzer-Regiment*, consisting of *9*

---

1 Most probably the Ju 87 G2 aircraft from *10 (tank-destroyer) Staffel* of the *Schlachtgeschwader 2* were deployed against the Soviet armoured fighting vehicles in the Bajna area. It might not be completely impossible though that the soldiers of the *3. SS-Panzer-Division* saw twin-engine aircraft resembling the Ju 88 over Bajna. In that case, those must have been the Hs 129 B2s of *14. Staffel* from *Schlachtgeschwader 9*. (Editor's note)

*Kompanie* (Tiger) and the Panthers from *I./SS-Panzer-Regiment 3*, fought their way through Gyarmatpuszta and then attacked Gyermely. During the day the Panthers engaged several Josef Stalin heavy tanks[2], with cover provided by two Tigers from *9 Kompanie*.

## 5 JANUARY 1945

THE *PANZERGRUPPE* UNDER THE LEADERSHIP of *SS-Obersturmbannführer* Laackmann advanced through Gyermelypuszta towards Szomor from the north-west. The Panzers of *SS-Panzer-Regiment 3* encountered strong Soviet tank and anti-tank gun defences. During the fighting, *SS-Obersturmbannführer* Laackmann was badly wounded. *SS-Sturmbannführer* Kraas, the former commanding officer of the self-propelled *I. Abteilung* of *SS-Panzer-Artillerie-Regiment 3*, was appointed as the new *Panzer-Regiment* commander. During the fighting for Szomor, the Panthers and Tigers managed to advance 2km west of Szomor, near Hill 289. The Panthers were then resupplied with fuel and ammunition. *SS-Untersturmführer der Reserve* Leciejewski was transferred from the *SS-Panzer-Ausbildungs- und Ersatz-Regiment* to the adjutant's office of the *SS-FHA* in Berlin. During the day, *SS-Untersturmführer der Reserve* Steinegger was killed in action.

## 6 JANUARY 1945

THE *PANTHER-ABTEILUNG* TOOK UP DEFENSIVE positions south-west of Szomor. During *Operation 'Konrad'*, many of the damaged Panzers of *SS-Panzer-Regiment 3* were towed to Tata and then sent by rail transport to Ács where the *IV. SS-Panzerkorps* had its *Werkstatt-Kompanie* set up in the grounds of a sugarcane processing factory.

## 7 JANUARY 1945

AT 0700 HOURS *SS-PANZER-ARTILLERIE-REGIMENT 3* opened fire with a barrage which lasted one hour; at 0800 hours the *Kampfgruppe*n began their advance on Zsámbék from the direction of Szomor.

With 10 Panthers, the *I./SS-Panzer-Regiment 3* tried to outflank Soviet positions south of Szomor to advance past Hill 317. The Panthers reached Felsőörspuszta-Esztermajor-Mány road junction where they were brought to a standstill by heavy Soviet defensive fire from the 382nd Guards Self-Propelled Artillery Regiment equipped with SU-100 self-propelled guns – the first time they had been used in combat. The 382nd Guards Self-Propelled Artillery Regiment had infantry in support but the Soviet riflemen quickly abandoned their positions leaving the

2 The JS-2 heavy tanks of Soviet 7th Mechanized Corps and even the JSU-122 heavy self-propelled guns of the Soviet 18th Tank Corps were also deployed in this area against the Panzers of *IV. SS-Panzerkorps*. (Editor's note)

SU-100 self-propelled guns without infantry cover. As the battle developed, some of the SU-100 self-propelled gun crews were forced to dismount to engage the *'Totenkopf'* grenadiers in close combat. The 382nd Guards Self-Propelled Artillery Regiment then signalled the 18th Tank Corps to request assistance and it responded by sending a tank battalion from the reserve to help the stranded 382nd Guards Self-Propelled Artillery Regiment. During the fighting one Panther was knocked out and nine sustained heavy battle damage. On the Soviet side, the 382nd Guards Self-Propelled Artillery Regiment lost 11 SU-100s. The Panthers encountered T-34 tanks and at least one Josef Stalin self-propelled gun, which was knocked out by a Panther from *3 Kompanie*.

During the heavy fighting, the crew of the Befehlspanther of *SS-Sturmbannführer* Kraas knocked out two Soviet tanks.

*SS-Rottenführer* Lindenau from *3 Kompanie* reported:

*'We were assigned a special task by* Obersturmführer *Herbatschek: we had to eliminate five Russian armoured fighting vehicles which were found in a valley with a Stalin assault gun among them.* SS-Unterscharführer *Sutter is the appointed commander of our Panther crew. At dawn we are on our way.*

*There is a flat Russian soldier lying on the road where the enemy armoured fighting vehicles retreated. We cannot go on a side track, so we also have to go over him. We take our position on the stated hill.* SS-Rottenführer *Wendland quickly stops the motor in order to prevent the Ivan from discovering us. Everything is in order except for one of the side slopes where our tank stands on the uneven terrain. It is beginning to dawn.*

*When we discover the five armoured fighting vehicles, I aim at the Stalin and shoot. "It's a hit!" However, I did not hit the Stalin but the T-34 standing at the edge of the wooded area and we did not see it before. I aim at the Stalin again. And again I hit the already burning T-34. Something is wrong with the aiming scope. We only discover much later that the sloped position of our tank itself was the problem. Now I aim my gun and align it to the tracer – even the first shot hits the chassis of the Stalin. The soldiers sitting on its rear run to cover. The next shot is a direct hit to its turret. Columns of smoke emerge from the hatches, then comes what is indescribable: the whole turret is blown off.*

*Meanwhile the crews of the other armoured fighting vehicles also react; they aim their guns at us and fire. We are hit on the right side; we have to change firing position. This is when driver Wendland reports that he is unable to start up the engine. That means a hit on the coupling! Now this is going to be uncomfortable for us. How to get out of here? We are trying...engine out, in reverse... start up starting-engine. With a shaky movement and downhill movement the starting-engine is able to move the vehicle so that the engine starts.*

*When we reach cover,* SS-Rottenführer *Wendland again stops the engine and tries the whole manoeuvre in first gear. In this way we stagger back to the command post...'*

**8 JANUARY 1945**

The *I./SS-Panzer-Regiment 3* along with the Panzer IVs from *5. Kompanie* were placed in reserve in Szomor while *6.* and *7. Kompanien* of *II./SS-Panzer-Regiment 3* supported two battalions from *SS-Panzergrenadier-Regiment 6 'Eicke'* in an attack on Mány.

**9 JANUARY 1945**

The *Panther-Abteilung* remained in the area of Szomor until 13 January 1945. New orders were issued for redeployment into the area of Berhida. *SS-Panzer-Regiment 3* was to be entrained in Komárom and moved to Veszprém by rail.

**10 JANUARY 1945**

The *I./SS-Panzer-Regiment 3* was still covering defensive positions in the area of Szomor. A small number of replacements arrived for *SS-Panzer-Regiment 3* and were divided between *I.* and *II./SS-Panzer-Regiment 3*. Included in the new intake was *SS-Unterscharführer* Hans Fenn who had just recovered from wounds. Fenn was placed in command of the *Kradmelder-Staffel* (motorcycle dispatch rider unit) for *I./SS-Panzer-Regiment 3*. Hans Fenn had originally served as a Panzer commander (Panzer IV 616) in *II./SS-Panzer-Regiment 12* in Normandy and had been wounded when his tank was knocked out near Buron. When Hans Fenn arrived at the command post of *SS-Panzer-Regiment 3* he was told that when a position became available he could opt for either a Panzer IV or Panther as a tank commander.

Hans Fenn: *'Naturally I opted for the Panther tank – better life insurance after my experience with a Panzer IV.'*

**11 JANUARY 1945**

*SS-Sturmbannführer* Pitschellis was given command of *SS-Panzer-Regiment 3* and *SS-Sturmbannführer* Kraas was transferred to assume command of *SS-Panzerjäger-Abteilung 3*.

**12 JANUARY 1945**

The *SS-Totenkopf* divisional headquarters informed *SS-FHA* in Berlin of *SS-Sturmbannführer* Meierdrees' death. The *I./SS-Panzer-Regiment 3* was temporarily subordinated to the *I. Kavallerie-Korps*. The *Abteilung* returned to the control of *SS-Panzer-Regiment 3* on 13 January 1945.

**13 JANUARY 1945**

The *I./SS-Panzer-Regiment 3* moved to Komárom to entrain for transfer south and redeployment in the area of Berhida.

## 16 JANUARY 1945

Frau Meierdrees received formal notification of her husband's death via the SS Supreme Command Office in Berlin. *SS-Obersturmführer* von Kleist was awarded the German Cross in Gold.

## 17 JANUARY 1945

The rail transports carrying *I./SS-Panzer-Regiment 3* arrived in Veszprém. After unloading, the *Panther-Abteilung* moved by road into the new assembly area in the vicinity of Berhida. The *IV. SS-Panzerkorps* reported to *Armeegruppe Balck* that only eight Panthers (two Panthers were still in long-term repair) from *I./SS-Panzer-Regiment 3* had so far arrived with another 14 due to arrive soon. With regard to the rest of the division, the following had still not arrived in the new assembly area: 11 Tigers from *9 Kompanie*, 16 Panzer IVs and six StuG. IIIs from *II./SS-Panzer-Regiment 3*, five Jagdpanzer IVs and six Stug IIIs from *SS-Panzerjäger-Abteilung 3* and five *Panzerspähwagens* from *SS-Panzer-Aufklärungs-Abteilung 3*. Also, the *I./SS-Panzer-Artillerie-Regiment 3* had not turned up nor had two towed artillery guns from the *II./SS-Panzer-Artillerie-Regiment 3* and one Flak 8.8cm and two 3.7cm guns were still un-accounted for by *SS-Flak-Abteilung 3*. In addition to these shortfalls, the division was still awaiting the arrival of a battalion of *Panzergrenadiere*.

## 18 JANUARY 1945

The Befehlspanthers from the *Stabskompanie* of *SS-Panzer-Regiment 3* led the advance eastwards from Küngös. *SS-Sturmbannführer* Pitschellis was at the point. Driving alongside the lead Panthers was the *Panzer-Pionierzug* from *I./SS-Panzer-Regiment 3* which was under the command of *SS-Untersturmführer* Mink. Also nearby was *SS-Kampfgruppe Kleffner* (*SS-Obersturmbannführer* Kleffner, commanding officer of *SS-Panzergrenadier-Regiment 6 'Eicke'*). The Panthers of *I./SS-Panzer-Regiment 3* tried at first to cross the Malom and Nádor Canals near Falubattyán and Szabadbattyán but were forced back by heavy Soviet anti-tank gunfire. Attached to *SS-Panzer-Regiment 3*, was *s.Pz.Abt. 509* with 45 new King Tigers. The *Kradmelder-Staffel* of the *Panther-Abteilung* (under the command of *SS-Unterscharführer* Fenn) was attached to the *Tiger-Abteilung*. The Soviets reported 20 Panzer IVs and Tigers advancing on their positions. Meanwhile, the remaining 14 Panthers that had been in transit arrived and were unloaded in Veszprém.

*SS-Oberscharführer* Steiger reports:

*'Then we had to move again, this time in to the Balaton area and then drive across ice-covered roads into the new assembly area. The new attack began on 18 January at 0430 hours. We encountered electrical cables, charged obstructions and mine fields. The Russians defended doggedly and the breakthrough was only achieved*

*in the evening. Székesfehérvár was captured on 21 January 1945 but our losses were high: Lischewski, Grimminger and Krohan were all killed; Hans Eggert was badly wounded and lost the sight of one eye. We reached the Vál sector on 25 January and on 29 January the Russians attacked our flanks. Soon, we were engaged in a large-scale tank battle near Pettend and some 200 Russian tanks were destroyed. The Russians increased their attacks on 30 January; we could no longer hold and so we withdrew westwards, on both sides of the Velence Lake. Budapest fell to the Russians on 12 February. Earlier in the month* SS-Obersturmbannführer *Laackmann had been wounded. The* Kompanie *had two Panthers left, one of which was commanded by* SS-Unterscharführer *Reif; the other Panther was commanded by an NCO from* 3 Kompanie. *All the other commanders were either dead or wounded.'*

## 19 JANUARY 1945

A BRIDGE WAS BUILT OVER the Nádor Canal allowing the Panthers and Tigers of *SS-Panzer-Regiment 3* to continue their advance from the area of Seregélyes. The attached *s.Pz.Abt. 509* with its Tiger IIs had to wait because the bridge had a maximum weight load of 40 tons. During the day some nine Panthers fall out because of technical trouble or battle damage.

## 20 JANUARY 1945

AFTER ANOTHER DAY OF HEAVY fighting the *I./SS-Panzer-Regiment 3* entered Dinnyés. The Soviets reported a limited advance on Kisvelence with seven Panzers but the attack was beaten back. The Soviets claimed two Panzers knocked out or damaged with the loss of one anti-tank gun. *SS-Hauptsturmführer* Berlin took command of *I./SS-Panzer-Regiment 3* and *SS-Obersturmführer* Lummitsch resumed command of *4. Kompanie.*

## 21 JANUARY 1945

THE *I./SS-PANZER-REGIMENT 3* ADVANCED FROM Dinnyés north-east towards Agárd. Before heading towards Gárdony, the *Panther-Abteilung* came under Soviet anti-tank gunfire from the outskirts of Agárd. Later, while crossing the open terrain south of Gárdony heading towards Kápolnásnyék, the leading four Panthers entered a small ravine on the western edge of Kápolnásnyék. *SS-Sturmbannführer* Pitschellis was at the point with his Befehlspanther along with one other Befehlspanther from the regimental *Stabskompanie.* All four of the Panthers were knocked out when they came under murderous Soviet anti-tank gunfire from the south and south-east of their positions. On 21 January 1945, *SS-Panzer-Regiment 3* lost two Befehlspanthers (from the regimental *Stabskompanie*) and two other Panthers (one of these from *1. Kompanie*). The four Panther wrecks were not recovered (for scrap) until 1950 by the Hungarian authorities.

At 0600 hours, the Soviets reported that *SS-Panzer-Regiment 3* had advanced with 25 operational Panzers in a south-easterly direction before moving towards Kisvelence and Kápolnásnyék. German forces tried to capture the crossroads just south of Kápolnásnyék. On 21 January 1945, the Soviets claimed eight Panzers knocked out or damaged and one SPW knocked out for the loss of 12 anti-tank guns from the 1,008th Separate Anti-Tank Artillery Regiment.

**22 JANUARY 1945**

The Panthers immobilised in the fighting on 21 January 1945 were recovered and towed to the workshops for repairs. Those Panthers still in working order took part in heavy fighting for Kápolnásnyék but, due to heavy Soviet defensive fire, the attack came to a standstill.

**23 JANUARY 1945**

Supported by two battalions of grenadiers, at 1100 hours the *I./SS-Panzer-Regiment 3*, together with *I./Panzer-Regiment 24* (Panthers), renewed the attack on Kápolnásnyék. The Soviet side claimed a total of 15 Panzers destroyed during this action.

**24 JANUARY 1945**

Elements of *I./SS-Panzer-Regiment 3* and the *1. Panzer-Division*, *I./Panzer-Regiment 24* (Panthers) and *s.Pz.Abt. 509* (Tiger IIs) were organized into three assault groups with a total of 35 operational Panzers. All three *Kampfgruppen* launched an attack in the general direction of Baracska at 1100 hours. By 0100 hours on 25 January 1945, German forces were in Kápolnásnyék and the south-eastern edge of Baracska. The *I./SS-Panzer-Regiment 3* claimed the destruction of two Soviet tanks and two self-propelled guns that day.

**24/25 JANUARY 1945**

The few remaining operational Panthers were situated in Kápolnásnyék.

**25 JANUARY 1945**

The *I./SS-Panzer-Regiment 3* came under sporadic Soviet airstrikes. During the day, the *I./SS-Panzer-Regiment 3* also took part in a tank battle near Pettend. Also, two Panthers from the *Panther-Abteilung* tried to attack along the Kápolnásnyék-Baracska road on 25 January 1945.

**26 JANUARY 1945**

SS-*Kampfgruppe* Pitschellis launched another attack from the area of Pettend to try to reopen the Vál sector. In support were *I./Panzer-Regiment 24* (Panthers) and *s.Pz.Abt. 509* (Tiger IIs). *SS-Sturmbannführer* Pitschellis' Befehlspanther was immobilised by Soviet anti-tank gunfire. As *SS-Sturmbannführer* Pitschellis tried to exchange Panthers he was seriously wounded. *SS-Hauptsturmführer* Balzer assumed command of the Panzer regiment (*SS-Hauptsturmführer* Balzer remained with Panzer regimental *Stab* for the rest of the war). The *1. Kompanie* was taken over by *SS-Untersturmführer* Müller. Later in the day a single Panther supported German forces fighting near Kajászószentpéter. Soviet forces reported at least 26 Panzers forming up south of Baracska. A number of dispatch riders from the *Panther-Abteilungs Stab* were attached to *s.Pz.Abt. 509*.

*SS-Unterscharführer* Hans Fenn recalled:

*'On 26 January 1945,* Kampfgruppe *Pitschellis began the battle with the task of reopening the area of Vál and Vereb. My motorcycle section was attached to the Army's* 509 Tiger-Abteilung. *I remember riding behind a King Tiger with the commander standing in the turret. Suddenly the turret was hit by an anti-tank round with splinters flying everywhere. One of the splinters killed the King Tiger's commander. Luckily for me and my motorcycle section, we suffered no losses that day.'*

## 27 JANUARY 1945

THE *I./SS-PANZER-REGIMENT 3* WITH THREE Panthers took up defensive positions along the Vereb-Pázmánd road, providing cover for the withdrawal of *SS-Panzergrenadier-Regiment 6 'Eicke'*. In the area of Kápolnásnyék, Soviet ground-assault aircraft launched airstrikes in the area of the village while a Panther situated in the village was hit and damaged by Soviet tank fire. The maintenance officer for *Armeegruppe Balck* reported on the various conditions of the Panzer units assigned to *Heeresgruppe Süd* (Army Group South). Regarding *SS-Panzer-Regiment 3*, the maintenance officer found that the maintenance service of this regiment was one of the best, with an officer inspecting all damaged Panzers before and after repairs. On 27 January 1945, the *I./SS-Panzer-Regiment 3* received 11 new engines for its Panthers. Also, a large rail transport carrying spare parts was expected but there was as yet no confirmed date for the arrival of this transport. He also reported that the recovery platoons with the Bergepanthers were working very effectively.

## 28 JANUARY 1945

THE *CHEF* OF *1 KOMPANIE*, *SS-Untersturmführer* Müller, was killed by a Soviet airstrike on Gárdony. The Soviet 10th Air Assault Corps had launched Il-2 and A-20 Boston aircraft to conduct airstrikes on Gárdony, dropping FAB-100 and PTAB bombs. The Soviets reported seeing two Panzers in Gárdony that day.

In another report by *Heeresgruppe Süd* on the condition of the Panzer units, it was recommended that at least six Panzer units should receive a full replenishment of armoured vehicles, if not at least an allocation of vehicles which would allow the units to be brought up to 30% of authorized strength. For *I./SS-Panzer-Regiment 3* this would have meant a new issue of 10 Panthers. *SS-Obersturmführer* Lummitsch assumed command of a combined *Panther-Kompanie*, after *1.*, *2.*, *3.* and *4. Kompanie* were finally integrated into a single *Kampfgruppe*. The new *Kompanie-Spiess* was *SS-Hauptscharführer* Pehl.

## 29 JANUARY 1945

THE *I./SS-PANZER-REGIMENT 3* WAS INVOLVED in defensive fighting along with *9. Kompanie* (Tigers), north of Kápolnásnyék. In Gárdony, a single Panther and Tiger provided support to *I./SS-Panzergrenadier-Regiment 6 'Eicke'*.

*SS-Rottenführer* Lindenau of *3. Kompanie* reported the situation in Kápolnásnyék:

*'The battalion command post* [of the II./SS-Panzergrenadier-Regiment 5 'Totenkopf'] *is located in the village. The battalion is far short of its authorized strength. Leaving behind a Panzer guard, we spend the night alternately in a vaulted cellar. Hungarian women and girls who have fled from the Russians, are encamped here. They are all very upset.'*

## 30 JANUARY 1945

THE *I./SS-PANZER-REGIMENT 3* WAS STILL situated in Kápolnásnyék defending the division's flank against Soviet attacks. The *Panther-Abteilung* came under heavy Soviet airstrikes and a single Panther (Panther 333) from *3. Kompanie* is struck in the rear, blowing all the hatches. All the available operational Panthers were positioned among the houses in Kápolnásnyék. Occasionally the Soviets took shots with anti-tank rounds hoping to hit the odd Panther. During a snowfall, the Soviets launched an attack with the support of tanks. The Panthers responded with a limited counterattack and knocked out two Sherman tanks. *SS-Hauptsturmführer* Berlin was promoted to *SS-Sturmbannführer*.

*SS-Rottenführer* Lindenau from *3 Kompanie* reports on the situation around Kápolnásnyék:

*'At the early morning briefing at the headquarters of* SS-Hauptsturmführer *Bachmann, we are informed that the Russian machine gun nests are proving to be a problem for the grenadiers; we did not know – but found out later – that the Russians have tanks in the area. We move, initially accompanying the grenadiers; we recognise the Russian machine gun positions. We start battling the Russian machine gun nests along with the grenadiers using machine-gunfire and shells. All of a sudden a shell gets stuck in the breach; I talk quickly with the loader and we decide to unload the shell from*

*the breach using the ejector – our luck holds. After a few breathless seconds we open a hatch but bullets are flying around the turret. A stray splinter hits me on the chin. Later we spot seven Sherman tanks but they stay out of range and we cannot shoot at them.*

*Our Panther is positioned near a house which we use for cover. The Russians are firing high explosive rounds known as "cap bombs" at us. The first watch falls to the radio operator Jupp Hille. The increased shelling wakes us from our sleep, we rush out of the house to see what is happening, and the shells are falling in the snow. We climb onto the Panther and find Jupp fast asleep,* SS-Unterscharführer *Sutter and I drag Jupp out of the cupola. Jupp wakes up, and we can hear the Russians cursing. IVan had taken advantage of the snow to use as cover and they had almost gotten past us. Except for our driver we took up our positions.* SS-Unterscharführer *Sutter is firing with his pistol, the driver,* SS-Rottenführer *Wendland, has to use a hammer which he stows outside of the tank and smashes the ice around his hatch in order to open it. The Russian commander is using his pistol and throwing hand grenades in our direction. Suddenly we hear the sound of tanks, just as we did the previous evening. As the morning begins it seems we have a bright day ahead of us. Soon we discover the seven Sherman tanks – two of them had literally driven up to the outskirts of the village with another following behind. Looking through the gun sight I can see that the Russian tanks have not spotted us. I fire at the first tank and then the second tank. The Russian crew bail out of their stricken tanks and fall into the snow and disappear out of sight.'*

*SS-Obersturmführer* Klemme was promoted to *SS-Hauptsturmführer* and transferred to the regimental *Werkstatt-Kompanie. SS-Untersturmführer der Reserve* Reitwiessner became the new *TFK* for *I./SS-Panzer-Regiment 3. SS-Untersturmführer der Reserve* Reitwiessner had served with the *'Totenkopf' Division* from September 1939. From 2 September 1939 to 10 October 1939 he served in *SS-Totenkopf-Standarte Prag* as an *SS-Unterscharführer* and from 10 October 1939 to 23 December 1941 he was attached to the *Stabskompanie* of the *I./Artillerie-Regiment 'Totenkopf'* as *SS-Scharführer*. From the 24 December 1941 to 31 August 1942 he served with the *SS-StuG.-Batterie 'Totenkopf'* as *SS-Oberscharführer* and from 1 September 1942 he served in the *1. Zug* of the *Werkstatt-Kompanie* of the *Panzer-Regiment* as an *SS-Hauptscharführer*. On 9 November 1943, he was promoted to *SS-Untersturmführer der Reserve* and transferred to *I./SS-Panzer-Regiment 3* but, before arriving at the *Panther-Abteilung*, he attended a *Kraftfahrzeugtechnischer Lehrgang* in Vienna.

### 31 JANUARY 1945

*SS-Obersturmführer* Ernst was ordered to form a collection detachment with 210 men to pick up new Panzers in Sennelager. One hundred and five of these men belonged to the *I./SS-Panzer-Regiment 3*. The group was sent to Veszprém to await transport by rail.

In Kápolnásnyék the *I./SS-Panzer-Regiment 3*, supported by the grenadiers from *II./SS-Panzergrenadier-Regiment 5 'Totenkopf'*, repelled another Soviet attack. During one attack a single Soviet Sherman was knocked out.

In January 1945, *SS-Untersturmführer* Ihrenfeldt was posted into the *Panther-Abteilung*. During January 1945 the Bergepanther platoons were working around the clock every day. One Bergepanther crew recovered 28 Panzers belonging to *SS-Panzer-Regiment 3*. These Panzers either had battle damage or had suffered some technical failure.

*SS-Rottenführer* Lindenau spoke about his Panther in Kápolnásnyék:

*'In the dark we arrive at our new location. Jupp Hille gets out to guide the driver,* SS-Rottenführer *Wendland. SS-Wendland kills the engine and we can hear the unmistakable "tak-tak"noise made by the "lame duck" aircraft – and then the whizzing of a falling bomb. The Russian pilot must have spotted the flames from the Panthers exhaust pipes. The bomb falls about half a metre behind our Panther. One of the hatches is open and we decide to get the hell out – if the hatch had been closed we could have suffocated from the pungent fumes. Our radio operator, Jupp Hille, is trying to work on the engine compartment and he is screaming that he needs help with the work but another bomb falls and comes crashing down nearby. Jupp takes cover underneath the Panzer but he loses his life as he is hit by bomb splinters.'*

## 1 FEBRUARY 1945

The *I./SS-Panzer-Regiment 3*, while still in Kápolnásnyék, fought off a Soviet attack in company strength with the support of tanks. The Panthers and the grenadiers held their positions. South of Székesfehérvár, the bulk of the *SS-Totenkopf* division started to move north of Székesfehérvár while *I./Panzer-Regiment 24* (Panthers) was temporarily attached to *SS-Panzer-Regiment 3* again.

## 2 FEBRUARY 1945

Early in the day, *I./SS-Panzer-Regiment 3* saw some limited action just to the north-east of Kápolnásnyék. During the night the *I./SS-Panzer-Regiment 3*, along with other elements of the division, withdrew from Kápolnásnyék.

## 3 FEBRUARY 1945

There were no operational Panthers – all 17 tanks were undergoing repair.

## 4 FEBRUARY 1945

Elements of *Kampfgruppe Lummitsch* were involved in some limited action after three Panthers returned to service and attached to the *5. SS-Panzer-*

*Division 'Wiking'*. These three Panthers were sent to Csiribmajor to support *SS-Panzergrenadier-Regiment 9 'Germania'* and guarded the road between Csiribmajor and Pálmajor. One Panther was located 300 metres north-east of Csiribmajor with the remaining two Panthers positioned either side of the road leading to Pálmajor.

**5 FEBRUARY 1945**

THE *I./PANZER-REGIMENT 24* (PANTHERS) LEFT the control of *SS-Panzer-Regiment 3*. Also on this day, Befehlspanther I01was written off as a total loss.

**6 FEBRUARY 1945**

THE THREE PANTHERS WERE STILL attached to the *5. SS-Panzer-Division 'Wiking'*. The Soviets launched five attacks during the day in the area between the Nádor Canal and the railway line (Seregélyes-Székesfehérvár). Seven or eight Soviet tanks were knocked out and the Panthers were later moved to defend a gap near Jánosmajor. The *5. SS-Panzer-Division 'Wiking'* tried to defend the road between Börgönd and Székesfehérvár. In the evening, the three Panthers were joined by another Panther which had just returned after repair.

**7 FEBRUARY 1945**

THE *I./SS-PANZER-REGIMENT 3* ALONG WITH elements of *1. Panzer-Division*, launched a local counterattack to the west of Jánosmajor in order to close a gap in the Margarethen Line. The Panthers were supported by *Panzer-Artillerie-Regiment 73* from the *1. Panzer-Division*. The Panthers from *I./SS-Panzer-Regiment 3* had been dispatched to the *1. Panzer-Division* at 0200 hours on 7 February 1945. The general direction of the counterattack was towards Hill 130. The Soviet 521st Separate Anti-Tank Artillery Regiment lost all its 76mm guns.

**8 FEBRUARY 1945-9 FEBRUARY 1945**

THE *PANTHER-ABTEILUNG* WENT OVER TO the defensive south-west of Dinnyés in readiness for a Soviet attack.

**10 FEBRUARY 1945**

MORE LOCAL COUNTERATTACKS TOOK PLACE in the area of Jánosmajor and attempts were made to reach Hill 151.

**12 FEBRUARY 1945**

AFTER THE RECENT BATTLES OF January 1945, the wounded from *I./SS-Panzer-Regiment 3* were sent to Veszprém or Réde, near Kisbér, to recover.

**13 FEBRUARY 1945**

*SS-Hauptsturmführer* Martin took command of *I./SS-Panzer-Regiment 3.* *SS-Hauptsturmführer* Dr. Alfons Martin had originally studied Medicine from 1933 in Frankfurt and entered the SS on 3 June 1933. Between January 1940 and May 1942 he served in various *Waffen-SS* medical units. On 24 July 1944 he was transferred to the *3. SS-Panzer-Division 'Totenkopf'* until the 10 October 1944 when he was posted to the *IV. SS-Panzerkorps*. He was promoted to *SS-Untersturmführer* on 20 April 1934, *SS-Obersturmführer* on 20 April 1941 and to *SS-Hauptsturmführer* on 30 January 1943.

**15 FEBRUARY 1945**

*SS-Obersturmführer* Ernst and the 210-man collection party left Veszprém for Sennelager-Augustdorf, Nordlager in Germany.

**18 FEBRUARY 1945**

The collection party from *SS-Panzer-Regiment 3* arrived in Sennelager-Augustdorf, Nordlager.

**22 FEBRUARY 1945**

The bulk of the *3. SS-Panzer-Division 'Totenkopf'* were redeployed to the north-west of Székesfehérvár, in the area of Magyaralmás. A rest area for the *Abteilung* was set up in Fehérvárcsurgó. The command post for *I./SS-Panzer-Regiment 3* was situated in Magyaralmás along with a reporting centre in the middle of the village.

**23 FEBRUARY 1945**

The *I./SS-Panzer-Regiment 3* reported that the day was spent quietly with no enemy activity along its front.

**25 FEBRUARY 1945**

Soviet infantry escorted by tanks attacked the *3. SS-Panzer-Division 'Totenkopf'* positions from the direction of Zámoly in regimental strength. The Panthers in Magyaralmás provided close support to the grenadiers and the Soviet attack was beaten back. Another Soviet attack north of Zámoly was also beaten back by an armoured group from the Hungarian 2nd Armoured Division.

**27 FEBRUARY 1945**

The *II./SS-Panzer-Regiment 3* set up an *Infanterie-Kampfgruppe* in Bakonyszentkirály under the command of *SS-Obersturmführer* Krutzenbichler from the *Versorgungs-Kompanie*. This battle group fought in the following areas: Jásd, Kóphaza, Sopron, Wiener Neustadt and Sankt Pölten, up to 3 April 1945.

## 1 MARCH 1945

THE *I./SS-PANZER-REGIMENT 3* SECTOR WAS quiet but, to the south, preparations were under way for *Operation 'Frühlingserwachen'*(Operation Spring Awakening).

The *I./SS-Panzer-Regiment 3* still had 915 men on strength. During February 1945, half of the Panthers remained in repair because of chronic shortages of spares (especially engine parts), engine damage (sustained by the use of poor quality manufactured fuel) and the lack of a 6-ton boom-arm crane vehicle suitably mounted for lifting and lowering engines.

*SS-Unterscharführer* Fenn was finally assigned a Panther tank which had belonged to *3 Kompanie*. It is possible that *SS-Untersturmführer der Reserve* Dr. Abt was posted to *SS-Sanitäts-Ausbildungs- und Ersatz- Bataillon* in Stettin but alternatively he might have remained with *I./SS-Panzer-Regiment 3*.

## 6 MARCH 1945

THE *I./SS-PANZER-REGIMENT 3* WAS STILL situated in Magyaralmás. In Mór, rail transports arrived carrying new spare parts for the Panthers – these had been requested at the end of January. Also elements of the Hungarian 2nd Armoured Division launched limited attacks in the area of Csákberény with *SS-Panzer-Regiment 3*. The Soviets reported about 30 armoured vehicles being used in this attack.

## 7 MARCH 1945

THE SOVIETS REPORTED AN ATTACK with 16 Panzers and about 130 German troops in the areas of Felsőpuszta ands Csákberény. The *I./SS-Panzer-Regiment 3* sent three Panthers to the north of Magyaralmás to support Hungarian infantry from the Hungarian 2nd Armoured Division in the area of Csákberény. Two Tigers from *9. Kompanie* were present at the industrial facility in Orondpuszta.

Hans Fenn recalled:

*'After one week I'm sent back to the front with my Panther as part of a group of three Panthers. We are to provide support to some Hungarian infantry in the front line. We had been positioned near Magyaralmás where we spent some cosy days with the Hungarian infantry at the front. My Panther is in cover behind a brick wall.'*

## 8 MARCH 1945

*SS-HAUPTSTURMFÜHRER* MARTIN WAS STILL IN command of *I./SS-Panzer-Regiment 3*. The Soviets used heavy artillery fire on various *SS-Totenkopf* divisional front line positions. The *IV. SS-Panzerkorps* ordered *3. SS-Panzer-Division 'Totenkopf'* to launch a limited attack in the direction of Lovasberény and advance as far as the woods 3km west of Pátka. The *6. Panzer-Division*, *5. SS-Panzer-Division*

*'Wiking'* and the Hungarian 2nd Armoured Division were assigned to the *IV. SS-Panzerkorps* which had given the various divisional units four days to complete their tasks. On the same day, all Panther tank crews without tanks were formed into an *Infanterie-Kampfgruppe.*

### 9 MARCH 1945

The *I./SS-Panzer-Regiment 3* reported its sector as being very quiet that day.

### 10 MARCH 1945

Soviet artillery fire provided covering fire for a limited infantry counterattack north-east of Magyaralmás.

### 10/11 MARCH 1945

The *I./SS-Panzer-Regiment 3* was involved in limited actions straightening the divisional front line. The three Panthers near Csakberény were officially attached to *9. Kompanie.*

### 11 MARCH 1945

The Soviets shell the front lines of *3. SS-Panzer-Division 'Totenkopf'* between Magyaralmás and Sárkeresztes.

### 14 MARCH 1945

The *I./SS-Panzer-Regiment 3* was placed in the divisional reserve along with *I./SS-Panzergrenadier-Regiment 5 'Totenkopf' (gepanzert)*. Both units were in the area of Magyaralmás.

### 14/15 MARCH 1945

During the night, Soviet forces conducted reconnaissance missions against Magyaralmás and reported the presence of German Panther and Tiger tanks in the village. Also, just to the north of Magyaralmás, *SS-Panzer-Artillerie-Regiment 3* had placed 12 towed artillery guns from the *IV- (schwere) Abteilung.*

## 3.2. Withdrawal and Capitulation

Overview

After the German offensive *Operation 'Frühlingserwachen'* had been halted on 15 March 1945, the Soviets went over to the attack launching a series of large-scale attacks north and south-west of Székesfehérvár on 16 March 1945. The *3.*

*SS-Panzer-Division 'Totenkopf'* was attacked by the 9th Guards Army, north of Székesfehérvár, forcing the *'Totenkopf' Division* to withdraw to the north-west. The *'Totenkopf' Division* was split into three *Kampfgruppen*: one *Kampfgruppe* was attached to the *1. SS-Panzer-Division 'Leibstandarte Adolf Hitler'*, one *Kampfgruppe* was attached to the *12. SS-Panzer-Division 'Hitlerjugend'* with the third group remaining with the *'Totenkopf'* divisional *Kampfgruppe*. By the 30 March 1945, the *'Totenkopf' Division* had crossed the Austrian border from Hungary and then took part in the battle for Vienna during mid-April 1945.

## 16 MARCH 1945

The *I./SS-Panzer-Regiment 3* was placed under the command of *I./SS-Panzergrenadier-Regiment 5 'Totenkopf' (gepanzert)* by a divisional order. The battalion's assembly area was actually south of Magyaralmás, near Hill 257.

The operational Panthers belonging to the *Abteilung* were deployed as follows: four Panthers east of Magyaralmás near the front line; three Panthers slightly north of Magyaralmás to provide support to Hungarian infantry; one Befehlspanther at the *Abteilung* command post in Magyaralmás. The command post was located at the first house just off the road leading into the village. The forward *Panzer-Werkstattzug* from the regimental *Werkstatt-Kompanie* was based in Sőréd and returned two more Panthers to service which eventually brought the total number of Panthers in and around Magyaralmás to 10.

The Soviets forces launched a strong attack to the north of Székesfehérvár, beginning at 1500 hours with a massive artillery barrage lasting 30 minutes – some reports state 60 minutes. The 98th Guards Rifle Division of the 9th Guards Army was tasked with taking Magyaralmás and Borbálamajor. In the first wave of the attack the division committed the 296th Guards Rifle Regiment and the 302nd Guards Rifle Regiment, each with two battalions. During the second wave of the attack the 299th Guards Rifle Regiment was held in reserve.

The positions of *I./SS-Panzer-Regiment 3* came under heavy Soviet artillery fire. During the artillery strikes, *SS-Unterscharführer* Bohme in a Panzer IV (from *5 Kompanie*) was killed while trying to move his tank out of firing range. His driver was also killed. *SS-Untersturmführer* Connert was killed by artillery fire while trying to take cover near the *Abteilung* command post.

Sometime later, *SS-Obersturmführer* Engelbrecht (transferred from *II./SS-Panzer-Regiment 3*) becomes the new ordnance officer. At 1700 hours[3], the *I./SS-Panzer-Regiment 3* and *I./SS-Panzergrenadier-Regiment 5 'Totenkopf' (gepanzert)* launched a local counterattack against the 98th Guards Rifle Division. The attack was beaten back by strong Soviet defensive fire. The counterattack had at least

3 According local time in Moscow. (Editor's note)

two Panzer IVs from *5. Kompanie* in support. The main force had four Panthers with another Panther providing flank protection. As the main Panther group advanced along the south-east exit road towards Borbálamajor, all the Panthers were either knocked out or immobilised. At least one Panther managed to advance 1.5km east of Magyaralmás before getting stuck in the thick mud after which it was immobilised in the general area of Hill 225 by the 57mm anti-tank gunfire from the platoon of Guards Lieutenant Vladimir Bordrizenko of the 3rd Battalion of the 302nd Guards Rifle Regiment. As the Panther tried to manoeuvre it threw the right track forcing the crew to bail out and abandon the stricken Panther.

*SS-Hauptsturmführer* Bachmann, commanding officer of *III./SS-Panzergrenadier-Regiment 5 'Totenkopf'*, requested additional Panzer and grenadier support as his battalion came under heavy Soviet attacks on Csillakipuszta. Later, *SS-Hauptsturmführer* Bachmann was killed by Soviet artillery fire.

At 1800 hours[4] the 98th Guards Rifle Division reported another German counterattack on 296th Guards Rifle Regiment opposite its front, just east of Magyaralmás. The Soviets reported that this attack consisted of a battalion of grenadiers supported by at least 15 Panzers. At 1840 hours[5] the 2nd Battalion of the 322nd Guards Mortar Regiment fired a salvo of M-13 Katyusha rockets into the south church (Catholic Church) area on Fő utca (the High Street) where an infantry battalion and four Panthers had assembled.

At 2000 hours[6] another limited counterattack was launched against the 98th Guards Rifle Division; the division reported at least two counterattacks on Alsópuszta and another on Borbálamajor from the direction of Magyaralmás.

During the day the *Panzer-Werkstatt-Kompanie* returned two Panthers in short-term repair to service.

In the area of Csillakipuszta and Alsópuszta, the *3. SS-Panzer-Division 'Totenkopf'* claimed five Soviet tanks knocked out. The three Panthers slightly north of Magyaralmás came under heavy artillery fire which caused communication difficulties between all three Panthers. After the barrage was over, Soviet infantry advanced towards the Panthers carrying anti-tank mines in wooden crates. The Panzer's on-board machine guns were used in attempt to keep the Soviet infantry at bay but one Panther sustained mine damage that caused the turret to jam. After a rapid inspection of the damage, the crew decided withdraw to Magyaralmás; the other two Panthers also withdrew towards Magyaralmás.

On arrival at their command post, where many of the soldiers who had fallen in battle had already been collected, the crew of the Panther with the damaged

4 According local time in Moscow. (Editor's note)

5 According local time in Moscow. (Editor's note)

6 According local time in Moscow. (Editor's note)

turret[7] reported that one of their comrades, *SS-Unterscharführer* Gratzer, had been killed and that their tank commander, *SS-Unterscharführer* Hans Fenn, had been wounded. A truck that had brought ammunition and spare parts from Mór was used to evacuate the wounded; it left Magyaralmás in the early hours of 17 March 1945 *en route* to a military hospital in Vienna. The wounded were first received in Schloss Schönbrunn Underground Station, then moved to a field hospital on Rosenhügelstrasse.

At the end of the day, the 98th Guards Rifle Division had only managed to advance 500 metres from its starting positions but they claimed to have captured 200 POWs and to have destroyed a Hungarian infantry battalion.

The Soviet 306th Air Assault Division launched 50 sorties with 24 Il-2 attack aircraft in the sector of the *3. SS-Panzer-Division 'Totenkopf'* but 13 of them were abandoned due to bad weather. The IL-2 Sturmoviks provided close air support to the advancing troops in the area of Sárkeresztes and along the road north to Bodajk. Nine major fires broke out when fuel depots in Mór and Bodajk were hit. The Il-2s were engaged by FW-190 fighters. The 306th Air Assault Division also claimed the destruction of one tank and 17 wheeled vehicles on this day.

Interestingly, the *Tiger-Kompanie* commander, *SS-Hauptsturmführer* Ther, reported that although the Panthers were hit hard by the Soviet infantry, the Tigers were more or less left alone. Ther shared quarters in a farm house with *SS-Hauptsturmführer* Martin just outside Magyaralmás.

*SS-Unterscharführer* Hans Fenn, a Panther commander, recalled the day's events:

*'On 16 March 1945 after a long artillery barrage we were forced to leave our excellent covering position as scores of Russian infantry came over the heights. In the heat of the moment we overlooked making radio contact with the other two Panthers because the Russian infantry were running at us carrying large wooden crates filled with anti-tank mines. They intend to get close and knock us out so we had to move. We fired into the throng of Russian infantry. I shouted at the driver, Sepp, to tell him to hit the gas and get us out of range of the Russians but they succeed in putting an anti-tank mine on the Panther. There was a loud bang. Suddenly we were unable to rotate the turret and the main gun was hanging over the side of the hull. We managed to put some distance between us and the Russians. We drove back to command post to inspect the damage. At the command post we found a lot of our dead already laid out. Of my own my crew;* SS-Unterscharführer *Gratzer was dead and I was wounded. A supply truck from the regiment bringing spare parts and ammunition was used for transporting the wounded to the clearing station. We were loaded onto the truck during the early morning hours on 17 March. In Vienna, I was put into the Rosenhügel Hospital.'*

7 This Panther was abandoned on Kossuth utca on 17 March 1945. (Author's note)

The Soviets reported the same event on 16 March stating that Guards Lieutenant Valentine Zhuzhokov, an anti-tank gun platoon commander, equipped with 57mm towed guns of the 296th Guards Rifle Regiment managed to hit two Panthers west of Zámoly and jam the turret of the third Panther forcing it to withdraw back into cover.

Franz Gschwandtner, from the *Berge-Staffel* of *I./SS-Panzer-Regiment 3* reported:
*'On 16 March, the Russian artillery opened fire on our positions. I was standing near the command post where SS-Obersturmführer Connert, the ordinance officer, was killed. After a huge artillery barrage, the Russian infantry launched an attack across the open terrain in three waves; luckily for us the ground was very soft and muddy and the Russian artillery had little effect.'*

*SS-Hauptsturmführer* Ther (commander of *9. Kompanie*) remembered:
*'During the early afternoon I had just sat down with* SS-Hauptsturmführer *Martin for lunch. The* Kompanie *cook had prepared my favourite meal and we were about to tuck in when the Russian artillery barrage opened fire. I looked at* SS-Hauptsturmführer *Martin and we went our separate ways – this was the last time I saw him alive.* SS-Hauptsturmführer *Martin had come from the army, he was a good comrade with an excellent sense of humour.'*

## 17 MARCH 1945

The order of the day for the Soviet 9th Guards Army was to destroy the German tank concentration in Magyaralmás within 24 hours.

Early that morning the Soviets conducted a massive air assault on the front line of the *3. SS-Panzer-Division 'Totenkopf'* while five Panthers from *I./SS-Panzer-Regiment 3*, escorted by a *Kompanie* of grenadiers from *I./SS-Panzergrenadier-Regiment 5 'Totenkopf'* (gepanzert), assembled in preparation for a local counterattack. The grenadiers mounted the Panthers leaving their SPW behind in Magyaralmás. As the advance began, an unfortunate grenadier fell from a Panther and became tangled in a track. As the Panthers attacked the right flank of the 296th Guards Rifle Regiment in the direction of Borbálapuszta during which they were supported by the *14. Kompanie* of *SS-Panzergrenadier-Regiment 5 'Totenkopf'* equipped with 2cm self-propelled Flak guns, one of which was soon knocked out.

Another 20 Panzers supported by a grenadier battalion attacked the left flank of the 296th Guards Rifle Regiment. Panzers from *II./SS-Panzer-Regiment 3*, managed to reach the edge of Borbálapuszta but heavy Soviet defensive fire forced the Panthers to withdraw back into Magyaralmás.

At 0640 hours, the *I./SS-Panzer-Regiment 3* with four Panthers and elements of *SS-Panzergrenadier-Regiment 5 'Totenkopf'* (with trucks) were seen assembling on the eastern edge of Magyaralmás by Soviet forward artillery observers. Soviet forces launched a Katshuya barrage which hit the assembly area forcing the German units to withdraw. The disposition of *SS-Totenkopf* Panthers in Magyaralmás at this time was as follows: two Panthers were on the eastern edge of Magyaralmás along with two Panzer IVs from *5 Kompanie*; two other Panthers were in the central part of the village.

At 0935 hours the *I./SS-Panzergrenadier-Regiment 5 'Totenkopf' (gepanzert)* and four Panthers reassembled near the Catholic church on Fő utca in the central part of the village. This time the Soviets responded with a 90-minute barrage of rockets fired by the 1st Battalion of the 322nd Guards Mortar Regiment. An infantry attack by the 296th Guards Rifle Regiment at 1030 hours failed. At 1100 hours a single Panther, originally from the northern edge of Magyaralmás, was firing at the attacking Soviet infantry just north of Magyaralmás while positioned on the main road leading from Székesfehérvár. At the same time another 10 Panzers and two battalions of grenadiers were observed at the eastern edge of the village. Again the Soviets launched a rocket salvo. About 30 minutes later, Soviet infantry from the 98th Guards Rifle Division (296th Guards Rifle Regiment), supported by a battalion from the 328th Guards Rifle Regiment (which in the meantime was attacking Magyaralmás to the north), joined the attack on Magyaralmás. The Soviets took several prisoners. The four Panthers near the church in the village were reportedly destroyed along with two SPWs which were also knocked out by rocket fire. Despite launching limited counterattacks in the direction of Borbálapuszta during the early morning, the *Panther-Abteilung* was forced to withdraw into Magyaralmás where it formed a perimeter defence around the command post which was soon destroyed by a direct hit from Soviet artillery fire, killing the commanding officer, *SS-Hauptsturmführer* Martin. The shelter for the crews of the Bergepanther was also hit. Several crew members were trapped are inside but they were eventually rescued by their comrades. On the main road from Székesfehérvár to Mór, a single Panther (see above) provided fire-support for the divisional *Begleit-Kompanie* as did an SPW with a 7.5cm short-barrelled gun (from *SS-Panzer-Aufklärungs-Abteilung 3*) and a StuG. from *SS-Panzerjäger-Abteilung 3*. These elements withdrew from the direction of Sőréd and retreated in the direction of Magyaralmás. The Panther fired high-explosive rounds into the oncoming Soviet infantry as they attacked across the open terrain.

Between 1130 hours and 1200 hours, the northern part of Magyaralmás was finally relinquished by the German forces and shortly afterwards, at 1230 hours, the Soviets reported the capture of large parts of Magyaralmás. The remaining elements of *I./SS-Panzer-Regiment 3* withdrew into Fehérvárcsurgó, where at about 1238 hours, three Panthers were attacked by Il-2 attack aircraft.

During the fighting near Hill 173, slightly north of Fehérvárcsurgó, Guards Lieutenant Valentine Zhuzhokov and his platoon again engaged Panthers from

*I./SS-Panzer-Regiment 3*. During the afternoon, the remaining elements of *I./ SS-Panzergrenadier-Regiment 5 'Totenkopf' (gepanzert)* – who were still holding the southern outskirts of Magyaralmás – were finally cleared by Soviet infantry at 1800 hours. Preparation for this infantry assault was provided by a salvo of rockets fired by the 3rd Battalion of the 322nd Guards Mortar Regiment.

The *I./SS-Panzergrenadier-Regiment 5 'Totenkopf' (gepanzert)* was forced to abandon 11 SPWs during its withdrawal from the village. After the fighting for Magyaralmás was over the Soviets recovered 13 SPWs, 22 light machine guns, two heavy machine guns, 12 mortars, one towed artillery gun, three bunkers and 13 Panzer wrecks in the area. In addition, three 'Nebelwerfer' rocket launchers were abandoned on the main road from Székesfehérvár to Mór (R81), just west of Magyaralmás.

After the war some children in Magyaralmás were playing with one of the 'Nebelwerfers' that had been left behind. The launcher was still loaded and they accidentally fired a rocket that hit the spire of the Reformed Church.

*I./SS-Panzer-Regiment 3* withdrew from Magyaralmás along the road leading to Igar, then made its way to Fehérvárcsurgó along the 8205 road. *SS-Obersturmführer* Lummitsch took command of the *Abteilung*.

At the end of the day on 17 March 1945, the 98th Guards Rifle Division had captured a total of 239 POWs and claimed to have destroyed a Hungarian infantry battalion and to have knocked out some 30 tanks and self-propelled guns in its area of operations. From the 16 March 1945 to 17 March 1945, this Guards Division reported losses of 228 men killed and 618 wounded.

On same day, the 306th Air Assault Division reported attacking Magyaralmás and Moha, hitting troop concentrations in Magyaralmás. Their claims for the day included five Panzers, 13 wheeled vehicles and one Flak battery of heavy guns. Another Air Assault Division, the 136th, claimed eight trucks and four Panzers in the same sector. The 951st Air Assault Regiment of the 306th Air Assault Division flew sorties from 1238 hours to 1800 hours in the sector of *3. SS-Panzer-Division 'Totenkopf'*. After the fighting, and more or less up to August 1945, local farmers were still using SPWs for farm work and general transport. It seems that the Soviets took a dim view of this and stopped and confiscated all German vehicles still in use.

*SS-Oberscharführer* Oldenburg, the *Panther-Abteilung*s Chief Clerk, reported: *'During the battle the* Abteilung *was partially destroyed.'*

*SS-Hauptsturmführer* Ther from *9. Kompanie* remembered the fighting around Magyaralmás:

*'The fighting in and around Magyaralmás was intense, but for some reason the Russian infantry set about our Panthers with zeal as though they were a priority and my Tigers were almost left alone, which was curious to say the least.'*

Another veteran recalled:

*'In the area of the command post the commander of our* Abteilung *was killed. The Russian attack pushed us out of the village and back onto the main road from Székesfehérvár to Mór. We had to cross the rail line under intense Russian fire when we pulled back into Fehérvárcsurgó which was already on fire.'*

## 18 MARCH 1945

At 1000 hours Soviet forces resumed their assault on the *3. SS-Panzer-Division 'Totenkopf'* positions in Fehérvárcsurgó. The tankless crews, now fighting as infantry, suffered heavy losses during the fighting for the town. The last report was made in the diary of the *I./SS-Panzer-Regiment 3.*

In Fehérvárcsurgó, the divisional *Stab* formed a *Kampfgruppe* from the *I./SS-Panzer-Regiment 3, I./SS-Panzergrenadier-Regiment 5 'Totenkopf' (gepanzert)* and the divisional *Begleit-Kompanie.* The wounded were evacuated from the divisional command post.

Six SPWs from *I./SS-Panzergrenadier-Regiment 5 'Totenkopf' (gepanzert)* with about 50 men on board withdrawing into Fehérvárcsurgó had trouble moving across the open ground. Three SPWs became bogged down and had to be recovered using Maultier trucks from the *Nachschub-Zug* of the *Tiger-Kompanie* under the supervision of *SS-Untersturmführer* Barth.

After intense fighting, Fehérvárcsurgó was captured by Soviet forces at 1520 hours The divisional *Kampfgruppe* withdrews from Fehérvárcsurgó in the direction of Guttamási along the 8212 road.

In Fehérvárcsurgó the fighting had been so intense that 208 of the 298 houses in the village had been damaged in the fighting.

South of Fehérvárcsurgó, one of the Panthers which had originally been on the northern edge of Magyaralmás was fighting along the road heading to Mór when it was bogged down in the thick mud. A Bergepanther made an attempt to recover the Panther but it threw its left track and the crew had to abandon the vehicle due to heavy fire from Soviet forces. One of the Bergepanther crewmen stopped a Panther that had been heading towards Guttamási to collect a new load of fuel and ammunition and asked for assistance. The Panther commander promised to return with another Bergepanther and three hours later fulfilled his promise. The second Bergepanther hooked up with the stricken Bergepanther. Meanwhile the replenished Panther also hooked up with the bogged-down Panther which it finally successfully recovered. After the recovery of the Panther, the Bergepanther with a thrown left track was towed to the *Panzer Werkstatt-Kompanie.* Some of the Bergepanther crewmen were wounded during the day and were taken to the main medical clearing station at Veszprém before being transported by road to Pápa. In Pápa, the wounded were sent by train to Linz where at the end of the war they were arrested by the Americans. These personnel were released from American captivity in May 1947.

The other Panther which had originally been on the northern edge of Magyaralmás had withdrawn via Sőréd onto the R81 road where it joined the divisional *Begleit-Kompanie* along with a StuG III from *SS-Panzerjäger-Abteilung 3* and elements of *SS-Panzer-Aufklärungs-Abteilung 3*.

In the fighting around Sőréd, *SS-Panzerjäger-Abteilung 3* lost all its vehicles (seven Jagdpanzer IVs, eight StuGs and one *Bergepanzer III*. The *SS-Panzer-Aufklärungs-Abteilung 3* also lost a substantial amount of equipment. In total the Soviets found the following in Sőréd: 21 Panzers, 71 *Schwimmwagen*, 30 SPWs, two self-propelled anti-tank guns, and 70 other wheeled vehicles. A large maintenance facility in Sőréd also fell into Soviet hands. North of Sőréd the *3. Batterie* of the *I. (Sfl.)/SS-Panzer-Artillerie-Regiment 3* lost five Hummel self-propelled howitzers which were knocked out in an ambush.

Franz Gschwandtner remembers the day as follows:

*'Soon enough we got the call – we had to go and recover a bogged-down Panther. During the manoeuvre we threw a track, so we had to leave our own* Bergepanthers *and go find another* Bergepanthers *to help us out. We managed to find another* Bergepanthers *which helped pull the Panther out of the mud. Our own* Bergepanthers *was towed by the other* Bergepanthers, *but the Russians spotted us and fired mortar rounds in our direction. During the barrage I was wounded by shrapnel. My comrades helped me and took me to a clearing station and from there I was evacuated via Pápa to Linz.'*

Franz Gschwandtner's Bergepanther was later abandoned. The vehicles from the *Nachschub-Zug* from *9. Kompanie* of *SS-Panzer-Regiment 3* were pressed into service by the divisional *Feldgendarmerie-Kompanie* in order to evacuate the wounded from Fehérvárcsurgó. The Soviets reported that, during the fighting for Fehérvárcsurgó, the anti-tank gun crew of Sergei Nikolaou of the 296th Guards Rifle Regiment managed to jam the turrets of two Panthers forcing them to withdraw while Guards Lieutenant Sergei Shilov of the same regiment managed to jam the turret of a third Panther near Hill 173. For this action he was awarded the Order of the Red Star.

## 19 MARCH 1945

THE DIVISIONAL *KAMPFGRUPPE* WITHDREW FROM Guttamási, which was captured at around 1330 hours, and moved in the direction of Isztimér. During the day the remaining elements of the *Panther-Abteilung* withdrew along a pathway leading north from Isztimér to Balinka, just east of Hill 348. In Guttamási, three Panthers from *I./SS-Panzer-Regiment 3* launched a limited counterattack which was supported by artillery fire. The three Panthers come under direct fire by units of the 5th Guards Tank Corps. After the fighting in Guttamási was over, the Soviets captured elements of the *'Totenkopf'* divisional *Stab*. The Soviets found 384 *SS-Totenkopf* soldiers dead and took 39 POWs. Also captured were 93 motor vehicles, 62 Lorries, seven field cars, six towed artillery guns and three SPWs. The 98th Guards Rifle Division reported 139 killed and 444 wounded. Further north, the Soviets captured Bodajk and attacked Balinka. The Soviets later reported that they had knocked out six Panzer IVs from the Hungarian 2nd Armoured Division in Bodajk and destroyed 100 trucks on the road west to Balinka; the Soviets also captured 10 trucks and 12 SPWs.

## 20 MARCH 1945

THE *I./SS-PANZER-REGIMENT 3* AND *I./SS-PANZERGRENADIER-REGIMENT 5 'Totenkopf' (gepanzert)* withdrew to the west from the direction of Balinka. In Mecsér, *SS-Panzer-Regiment 12* with 35 operational Panzers and 10 self-propelled guns counterattacked Soviet forces and managed to advance 1km, bringing some relief to the withdrawing *SS-'Totenkopf' Kampfgruppen.*

## 21 MARCH 1945

THE *PANZER-WERKSTATT-KOMPANIE* OF THE *SS-PANZER-REGIMENT 3* abandoned its former location in Hajmáskér. Other *Werkstatt* units from the German Army and *Waffen-SS* also abandoned unrepaired Panzers. At the railway station in Hajmáskér, four Panthers were found on rail flat cars. A total of 70 Panzers and assault guns were found in Hajmáskér which was finally captured during the early morning hours on 22 March 1945. Near Csőszpuszta the Soviets entered another *Werkstatt* unit and reported six self-propelled guns and four Panzers captured intact.

## 23 MARCH 1945

THE WHEELED ELEMENTS OF *I./SS-PANZER-REGIMENT 3* were forced to abandon, blow up or roll their vehicles down the hilly slopes in the area of Pénzeskút, due to the lack of fuel and mechanical breakdowns. Also on 23 March 1945, forces from the *12. SS-Panzer-Division 'Hitlerjugend'* left behind six Panzers and 10 self-propelled guns on the eastern edge of Zirc.

## 24 MARCH 1945

THE *I./SS-PANZER-REGIMENT 3* ALONG WITH other divisional elements regrouped in Bakonybél. A Hungarian officer who was later captured by the Soviets stated that there was a large number of soldiers from the *'Totenkopf' Division* in the area of Bakonybél. From radio intercepts, Soviet Military Intelligence estimated around 8,000 *'Totenkopf'* divisional members in the Bakonybél area.

## 25 MARCH 1945

Those Panzers still requiring repairs, including three Panthers, were towed through Pápa along the road towards Marcaltő.

## 26 MARCH 1945

Withdrawal continued north of Pápa, along the road through Ihász heading towards Marcaltő

## 27 MARCH 1945

An *Infanterie-Kampfgruppe* from *I./SS-Panzer-Regiment 3* was fighting in the area just to the north of Marcaltő.

## 30 MARCH 1945

The *Infanterie-Kampfgruppe* of *I./SS-Panzer-Regiment 3* were engaged in limited combat in the area of Kóphaza, along with the *Infanterie-Kampfgruppe* from *II./SS-Panzer-Regiment 3*. Both *Kampfgruppen* withdrew across the Hungarian border into Austria and carried the withdrawal onwards through Deutschkreutz (Sopronkeresztúr). The *Infanterie-Kampfgruppe* from *I./SS-Panzer-Regiment 3* was in action in Walpersbach.

## 31 MARCH 1945

The *Infanterie-Kampfgruppe* from *I./SS-Panzer-Regiment 3* withdrew through Erlach in the direction of Lanzenkirchen. *SS-Untersturmführer* Mink, commander of the *Panzer-Pionierzug* of *I./SS-Panzer-Regiment 3*, was transferred to *SS-Panzer-Pionier Bataillon 3*. The *Panzer-Pionierzug* for the *II./SS-Panzer-Regiment 3* was also disbanded along with the *Pionierzug* from *SS-Panzer-Aufklärungs-Abteilung 3* and was assimilated into *SS-Panzer-Pionier-Bataillon 3* to form a new *2. Kompanie* of *SS-Panzer-Pionier-Bataillon 3*. The following NCO's were also integrated with the *2. Kompanie* of *SS-Panzer-Pionier-Bataillon 3*: *SS-Unterscharführer* Kreutzer, *SS-Unterscharführer* Pahl and *SS-Rottenführer* Hainbach.

After a week of fighting on foot, the *Infanterie-Kampfgruppe* along with *Versorgungs-Kompanie* regrouped in Lanzenkirchen. *SS-Obersturmführer* Lummitsch was confirmed as the commander of the *Panther-Abteilung* by a divisional order. On the same order it was decided to disband *I./SS-Panzer-Regiment 3* (some veterans' reports state this order wasn't issued until the 1 May 1945) and integrate the remaining elements, including the *Versorgungs-Kompanie*, into *II./SS-Panzer-Regiment 3*.

At this time, *SS-Panzer-Regiment 3* could still field four Panzer IVs, three Panthers, three Tigers, two StuG. III's and two Bergepanthers. The *Infanterie-Kampfgruppe* of *I./SS-Panzer-Regiment 3* took up positions near Pittental, along with the cadets from the military school in Wiener Neustadt. The combined *Kampfgruppe* was under the command of *Hauptmann* Koch. The *Kampfgruppe* from the military school had command and control of all units in the Lanzenkirchen area, as ordered by *SS-Oberstgruppenführer* Dietrich.

Other elements of *SS-Panzer-Regiment 3* withdrew north towards Mattersburg. The *Werkstatt-Kompanie* from SS-Panzer-Regiment 3, towing six tanks, withdrew through the Pitten Valley towards Ofenbach and Lanzenkirchen.

*SS-Oberscharführer* Steiger wrote:

*'We crossed the border between Hungary and Austria at Lake Neusiedler and followed the retreat to Lanzenkirchen, south of Wiener Neustadt. Here, the supply company was ordered into infantry duty. We took up positions at the canal together with the cadets of the officer school in Lanzenkirchen. Around early afternoon on Easter Sunday, the Russians took Lanzenkirchen. We could not hold the position and withdrew towards Wiener Neustadt.'*

## 1 APRIL 1945

SOME PARTS OF THE *KAMPFGRUPPE* and cadets from the Weiner Neustadt Officer Cadet School defended Erlach. At 1000 hours elements of the 99th Guards Rifle Division attacked Erlach from the north-west. By 1500 hours the village was in Soviet hands and so too were some officer cadets whom the Soviets noted were on average between 28 and 29 years of age. In Erlach, the Soviets reported capturing nine trucks, six MGs, four store houses, two 7.5cm anti-tank guns and 35 railway wagons.

The last remaining Panthers were still under repair with the *Werkstatt-Kompanie* of *SS-Panzer-Regiment 3*. Meanwhile, the *Infanterie-Kampfgruppe* of *I./SS-Panzer-Regiment 3* were in Lanzenkirchen but was forced to give up the village. The total strength of the *Kampfgruppe* formed from *I./SS-Panzer-Regiment 3* was now only around 200 men. A total of eight SS-men were killed in action during the fighting for Lanzenkirchen. The dead were buried in Blumau, north-east of Wiener Neustadt.

## 2 APRIL 1945

THE REMAINING TROOPS FROM OF *I./SS-Panzer-Regiment 3* withdrew from Lanzenkirchen and moved towards Fischau via Eyden. At Eyden, the *Infanterie-Kampfgruppe* of the *I./SS-Panzer-Regiment 3* fought a rearguard action against advancing Soviet forces, knocking out two T-34 tanks. German forces retreating from Eyden abandoned much of their equipment. Those elements of *I./SS-Panzer-Regiment 3 fighting in Fischau withdrew along with SS-Panzergrenadier-Regiment 2* and *SS-Panzer-Artillerie-Regiment 1* of the *1. SS-Panzer-Division 'Leibstandarte'* and the officer cadets from Wiener Neustadt. On the same day, Bad Fischau was captured at 1800 hours. In Bad Fischau, the Soviets reported the following as captured: 20 aircraft, 12 tractors, six trucks, 40 railway wagons and around 300 POWs.

### 3 APRIL 1945

Elements of *I./SS-Panzer-Regiment 3* (ear-marked for rehabilitation) were moved into the area west of Sankt Pölten along with other elements of the *Panzer-Regiment.*

### 4 APRIL 1945

Elements of *SS-Panzer-Regiment 3* saw action in the area of Pischelsdorf, repelling Soviet attacks. Three Panthers from *I./SS-Panzer-Regiment 3* moved through Götzendorf and were attached to *SS-Kampfgruppe* Kuhn from the *III./SS-Panzergrenadier-Regiment 5 'Totenkopf'* while one Panzer IV defended against Soviet attacks near Mannersdorf.

The wounded personnel from *I./SS-Panzer-Regiment 3* recovering in the hospital on Rosenhügelstrasse, and who were fit enough to serve, were attached to the *II. Bataillon* of the *Hitlerjugend* in Vienna. The average age of the *HJ* members was between 14 and 15 years of age. The *Kampfgruppe* engaged in house-to-house fighting in the district of Kahlenberg during the Battle of Vienna. On 12 April 1945, the *Kampfgruppe* withdrew over the River Danube, across the *Reichsbrücke.* The *Kampfgruppe* was supported by a 2cm *Flak Vierling* vehicle and one truck. On 8 May 1945 the *Hitlerjugend Kampfgruppe* with personnel from *I./SS-Panzer-Regiment 3* surrendered to the US forces in Steiermark. They were released from US captivity on 12 August 1945.

### 6 APRIL 1945

The bulk of *SS-Panzer-Regiment 3*, along with the supply units and crews without tanks, was in the area of Kronberg and Wolkersdorf. The *Versorgungs-Kompanie* from *SS-Panzerjäger-Abteilung* 3 was attached to *SS-Panzer-Regiment 3*. The operational elements of *II./SS-Panzer-Regiment 3* (*5. and 8. Kompanie*) and two Panthers were in action along the Simmeringer Hauptstrasse, the main road from Schwechat to Vienna, together with *SS-Flak-Abteilung 3* and *SS-Panzergrenadier-Regiment 5 'Totenkopf'*. On the same day, *SS-Obersturmführer* von Kleist, who had been recovering from his wounds at the *SS-Panzer-Ausbildungs- und Ersatz-Regiment* in Sennelager, was assigned to *SS-Panzer-Brigade 'Westfalen'*, and killed in action.

### 7 APRIL 1945

Fifty men from the former *Infanterie-Kampfgruppe* of *I./SS-Panzer-Regiment 3* (tankless crews), equipped with *Panzerfäuste* (hand-held recoilless anti-tank rockets) were in action in the area of the Vienna East Railway Station. During the fighting *SS-Untersturmführer* Ober was killed.

In the early phase of the fighting in Vienna, between 6 April 1945 and 8 April 1945, a few operational Panthers from *I./SS-Panzer-Regiment 3* were reported fighting in the city.

## 8 APRIL 1945

The bulk of *I./SS-Panzer-Regiment 3* took up positions in the area of Rohrendorf after crossing the bridge in Tulln which was blown up in the evening.

The retreat from the 30 March 1945 to 8 April 1945 took place along the line Kópphaza-Nagycenk-Deutschkreuz-St.Martin-Kirchschlag-Bad Schonau-Edlitz-Erlach-Lanzenkirchen-Edau-Bad Fischau-Baden-Klausen-Leopoldsdorf-Pressbaum-Sieghartskirchen-Judenau-Langendorf-Tulln and finally Rohrendorf bei Krems. This was more or less the same route that was taken by *9. Kompanie.*

## 10 APRIL 1945

In the village of Wieselburg, the remaining elements of the *Panther-Abteilung* set up quarters for rehabilitation and refitting, in readiness for a new delivery of tanks. *SS-Obersturmführer* Herbatschek was in command of the training programme. Herbatschek had just returned to duty after recovering from a wound to his right eye. The *II./SS-Panzer-Regiment 3* set up a command post in Sausenstein.

*SS-Unterscharführer* Hans Fenn recalled:

*'After a few days I was sent from the hospital to the II. Battalion of the Hitlerjugend in Vienna. As a tank soldier I had no experience of house-to-house fighting. During the fighting the Russians were using an air-raid shelter they had found in a garden from which they launched attacks. We had a Flak Vierling mounted on a truck which would fire from a corner and then quickly move back, this forced the Russians back only for a bit. One day we found a* Wehrmacht *officer who commanded a full* SPW-Kompanie, *but they had no Panzers to support them.'*

## 10/11 APRIL 1945

A single Panther from *SS-Panzer-Regiment 3* was in action along with two Panzer IVs from *5 Kompanie* of *SS-Panzer-Regiment 3* and five Panzer IVs from *SS-Panzer-Regiment 2* in Vienna. This Panther was commanded by *SS-Obersturmführer* Lummitsch but the driver was shot in the head by a member of the Austrian Resistance movement while the Panther was in hiding; he died instantly. The remaining Bergepanthers were now close to the Reichsbrücke.

## 12 APRIL 1945

A Panther returned to service after being repaired was in action near the *Reichsbrücke* in Vienna, along with a Panzer IV and a StuG. III. Later that day all three armoured vehicles were knocked out by Soviet tank fire. The tankless crews from *I./SS-Panzer-Regiment 3* were at this time fighting in the *Prater* district in Vienna.

## 12/13 APRIL 1945

During the night the remaining elements of the *'Totenkopf' Division* still fighting in Vienna crossed the Reichsbrücke. The only operational Panzers left in *SS-Panzer-Regiment 3* were two Tiger Is, one Tiger II and one Panther (with one Panther under repair).

*SS-Unterscharführer* Hans Fenn reported that:

*'We drove back in a civilian truck, over the Floridsdorf Bridge which had a huge hole in it caused by the Russian artillery fire. Suddenly the* Hitlerjugend *in the truck broke into song – they showed no fear.'*

The following list shows the officers and their posts/commands at this point in time:

| | |
|---|---|
| *Abteilungskommandeur*: | *SS-Obersturmführer* Lummitsch |
| *Adjutant*: | *SS-Obersturmführer* Strobl |
| *Versorgungs-Kompanie*: | *SS-Untersturmführer* Kaden |
| *Panzer-Werkstattzug*: | *SS-Obersturmführer* Reitwieser |

## 13 APRIL 1945

One more Panther was returned to service after extensive repairs. *SS-Panzer-Regiment 3* formed a new *Infanterie-Bataillon* from elements of *I.* and *II./SS-Panzer-Regiment 3* (the assembly area was in Pochlarn-Sausenstein). The training of this *Bataillon* was due to have been completed by 25 April 1945. The remaining two Panthers of *I./SS-Panzer-Regiment 3* were combined with two Tiger Is and a Tiger II of *9. Kompanie* under the leadership of *SS-Obersturmführer* Neff to form *SS-Kampfgruppe Neff* which was then moved to Rohrendorf bei Krems.

During the fighting in Vienna, *SS-Unterscharführer* Reif was wounded and this left *SS-Oberscharführer* Steiger as the only qualified tank commander in *1. Kompanie*. The *Versorgungs-Kompanie* of *SS-Panzer-Regiment 3* was located in Wieselburg along with other regimental support units.

*SS-Oberscharführer* Steiger reported the following:

*'The last actions took place at the foot hills of the Alps, near Sankt Pölten and Krems. The division took positions in the area of Krems and at last the troops managed to get*

*some much needed rest. There was a shortage of Panzers and limited training was given to new replacements from the Luftwaffe. During this time* SS-Unterscharführer *Reif was wounded leaving myself as the remaining Panzer commander in* 1. Kompanie *which was now attached to* SS-Kampfgruppe Neff. *The* Kampfgruppe *had five Panzers of which two were Panthers. We also had a Flak-Panzer platoon with three Flak Vierling mounted on US M4 Sherman chassis.'*

On the same day, *SS-Panzer-Kampfgruppe Langanke* from *SS-Panzer-Regiment 2* was attached to *SS-Panzer-Regiment 3*. The *Kampfgruppe* was commanded by *SS-Obersturmführer* Langanke, *Chef* of *2. Kompanie*, and was situated in Kirchberg am Wagram.

### 15 APRIL 1945

More crews without tanks from *SS-Panzer-Regiment 3* were formed into an *Infanterie-Kampfgruppe* and sent to the *1. SS-Panzer-Division 'Leibstandarte'*.

### 16 APRIL 1945

The *Infanterie-Kampfgruppe* from *SS-Panzer-Regiment 3* was in action in the general area of Sankt Pölten and fighting alongside *SS-Flak-Abteilung 1*. The *SS-Panzer-Regiment 3* – which was now situated in the area of Pochlarn, southwest of Melk – began the process of reorganization. The remaining operational Panthers were still situated in Rohrendorf bei Krems and acted as a tactical reserve.

### 17 APRIL 1945

All the *Kompanien* of the *Panther-Abteilung* were close to annihilation and unable to function as a coherent unit. Replacement personnel arrived after being transferred from the *Luftwaffe* and were sent to Wieselburg where they were formed into new crews but they received Panzer training only on a short-term basis. The current equipment of the *Kompanien* was basically rifles, hand grenades and machine guns.

*SS-Untersturmführer* Kaden was transferred to the *13. Kompanie* of *SS-Panzergrenadier-Regiment 2* from the *1. SS-Panzer-Division 'Leibstandarte'*. The *Versorgungs-Kompanie* was taken over by *SS-Oberscharführer* Wunsch.

### 25 APRIL 1945

A collection party from the *Panther-Abteilung* was formed and sent to Znojmo (Znaim) to collect a new issue of Panthers but the delivery never took place. During April 1945, *SS-Untersturmführer* Leciejewski returned to the *Panther-Abteilung*.

*SS-Oberscharführer* Steiger continues his account during this time:

*'The* Abteilung *is virtually disseminated, the* Kompanien *are shattered. The cooks, clerks and mechanics are all pressed into infantry service. We are still waiting for the collection command to return from Zniam (Znojmo) and Paderborn with new Panzers. We have some new recruits from the* Luftwaffe *who were transferred. They are placed under the command of* SS-Obersturmführer *Herbatschek and are located in Wieselburg. The new recruits are given limited tank training in the anticipation of the new tanks arriving.* SS-Obersturmführer *Herbatschek had just been released from hospital a few days ago after he lost his right eye due to a shell fragment.'*

The *SS-Kampfgruppe Neff* was still situated in Rohrendorf bei Krems with two Panthers, three Tigers and a *Flak-Zug* commanded by *SS-Oberscharführer* Stoff.

**30 APRIL 1945**

*SS-Obersturmführer* Strobl was transferred to *SS-Panzergrenadier-Regiment 6 'Eicke'* as the new regimental *Adjutant. SS-Obersturmführer* Lummitsch appointed *SS-Standartenoberjunker* Dieter Baumann as the new *Abteilung Adjutant.*

**1 MAY 1945**

According to surviving veterans, the order to disband *I./SS-Panzer-Regiment 3* did not occur until the 1 May 1945 when the *I./SS-Panzer-Regiment 3* was integrated with *II./SS-Panzer-Regiment 3* to form a new *Panzer-Abteilung.* However, *5. Kompanie* (Panzer IV) was reconstituted. Those crews designated to take over the new Panthers upon arrival were ordered to remain in Wieselburg. Much of the new organization took place on paper and *SS-Panzer-Regiment 3* – even up to the last day of the war – was still reporting the existence of separate *I.* and *II. Batallione* for *SS-Panzer-Regiment 3.*

**5 MAY 1945**

The *8. (StuG) Kompanie* of *SS-Panzer-Regiment 3* under the command of *SS-Obersturmführer* Rademacher was ordered to convert to a bicycle reconnaissance company. *SS-Obersturmführer* Lummitsch was awarded the Knight's Cross by divisional commander *SS-Brigadeführer* Becker with the award approved and countersigned by *SS-Oberstgruppenführer* Dietrich, commander of the *6. Panzerarmee.*

**6 MAY 1945**

The training crews (Panther) were still situated in Wieselburg under the command of *SS-Obersturmführer* Herbatschek while two Panthers remained in Rohrendorf bei Krems with *SS-Kampfgruppe Neff.*

## 7 MAY 1945

The last assembly of *SS-Panzer-Regiment 3* took place and final orders issued; the regiment was to move to the demarcation line via Sausenstein, Amstetten, Enns and Pregarten. *Kampfgruppe Neff* was ordered to move towards Krems from Rohrendorf bei Krems as a tactical reserve.

*SS-Oberscharführer* Steiger wrote:

*'The remaining Panzers were moved from Rohrendorf to Krems to take up positions on the Danube.'*

## 8 MAY 1945

During the day SS-*Kampfgruppe Neff* was in Krems and received orders to defend the withdrawal of the *3. SS-Panzer-Division 'Totenkopf'* as it moved towards the demarcation line. *SS-Kampfgruppe Neff* was to secure the rear of the division until 1700 hours and then withdraw from Krems.

The divisional leadership now suspected the Soviets had crossed the Danube River. Also, the last regimental message was issued by *SS-Sturmbannführer* Berlin: 'Germany has surrendered unconditionally.'

At 1700 hours *SS-Kampfgruppe Neff* withdrew from Krems with two Panthers, two Tigers and three *Flak-Panzers* and drove into Noehagen bei Krems. The Tiger II stayed behind in Krems. The last two Panthers were abandoned in Noehagen bei Krems but two Jagdpanzer IVs continued to Jaidhof and Gföhl from Rohrendorf bei Krems where they were abandoned; one inside and one outside the village, on the road to Eisengraben, along with an SPW. The two Tigers moved to Weinzierl am Walde where they were abandoned and an SPW was set on fire. From Noehagen bei Krems, the *Kampfgruppe* personnel made their way to Neumarkt im Mühlkreis via Zwettl (just south of Freistadt). The remaining two Bergepanthers were abandoned – one north of Krems in Rehberg and the other in Stratzing.

Again *SS-Oberscharführer* Steiger recalled:

*'In the early morning hours of 8 May, the Russians fired a salvo of heavy artillery which startled us from our sleep.* SS-Obersturmführer *Neff and* SS-Obersturmführer *Lummitsch were at the command post where they read the last regimental order: "Germany has unconditionally surrendered". We have been ordered to secure the withdrawal of the division and prevent a possible crossing by the Russians until 1700 hours. '*

On 8 May, the two *Kompanien* of *SS-Panzer-Pionier-Bataillon 3*, with the personnel from the disbanded *Panzer-Pionierzug* from *I./SS-Panzer-Regiment 3*, were stopped by US forces along the road to Linz and taken prisoner. *SS-*

*Kampfgruppe Langanke* moved about 1km north of Kirchberg and Wagram to Engelmannsbrunn and blew up their remaining Panzers in three different locations around the village. The order to blow up the tanks was given by the *Ia* of the *3. SS-Panzer-Division 'Totenkopf'*. As the order was being carried out, Panzers from the *Führer Grenadier Division* passed through Kirchberg and Engelmannsbrunn, heading west. Also on the roads heading west, *SS-Panzer-Aufklärungs-Abteilung 3* left some heavy *Panzerspähwagen,* an SPW and a variety of soft-skinned vehicles in Maigen and in the woods around Lichtenau and Scheutz.

## 9 MAY 1945

THE *SS-KAMPFGRUPPE NEFF* WAS QUARTERED in Neumarkt im Mühlkreis along with some support elements from the division. In Neumarkt, the 11th US Armoured Division disarmed the soldiers of *SS-Kampfgruppe Neff.*

*SS-Oberscharführer* Steiger reported:

*'On 9 May we left Krems at 1700 hours and went to join the supply company in Neumarkt. When we arrived we learned that the line had been pulled further back to the west. The bulk of the division was situated in the area of Pregarten. The Americans would not allow us to cross the demarcation line. In the meantime the Russians caught up with us and demanded that the Americans hand over the T-Division. An order by the Allies spelled out that all German troops in the US Zone would go into US captivity and all those in the Russian Zone would go into Russian captivity as of 8 May.* SS-Brigadeführer *Becker addressed the division one more time and mentioned his personal fate was sealed because the Americans had left all of the* 'Totenkopf' *Division to the Russians. The result of this was that a mass breakout during the night of 12/13 May was attempted. Alas this soon turned into a panic which caused people to be trampled on and driven over. A few did manage to escape to the west but the Americans managed to stop the bulk of the breakout with tanks and then began turning over the personnel to the Russians. Eyewitness later reported the march of misery eastward which lasted weeks. In captivity, the former members of* 'Totenkopf' *had to suffer denunciation, treachery, hunger and misery. Only after six years in Russian prisons did we return to Germany.'*

*SS-Unterscharführer* Hans Fenn ended the war as follows:

*'On 8 May 1945, I ended the war in Steiermark and I was taken prisoner by the English and released August 1948.'*

## 8/9 MAY 1945

THE *3. SS-PANZER-DIVISION 'TOTENKOPF'* ASSEMBLED in the area of Pregarten. Its support units were in the area of Neumarkt. Those elements of the *Panzer-Regiment* (with *SS-Panzerjäger-Abteilung 3*) acting as the advance party made contact with the 65th US Infantry Division. Attempts were made to surrender to US forces.

Franz Gschwandtner recalls:

*'On the last day of the war, I was captured by the Americans while still in hospital and put under "automatic arrest". I didn't return home until 1947.'*

**10 MAY 1945**

Soldiers from the *'Totenkopf' Division* were quartered in the area of Gallneukirchen by the Americans.

**12/13 MAY 1945**

During the night 8,000 or so soldiers of *3. SS-Panzer-Division 'Totenkopf'* attempted a night-time breakout towards the west. As the attempt began a few divisional soldiers managed to get across the American lines but very quickly US armoured units blocked the escape routes and regained control of the situation.

**14 MAY 1945**

The Americans turned over *SS-Totenkopf* personnel to the Soviets. For many former members of *I./SS-Panzer-Regiment 3* this was the start of a long period of imprisonment. The first release of former personnel formally of *I./SS-Panzer-Regiment 3* took place in 1951; the rest were released in 1955. The 11th US Armoured Division turned over 34,125 German POWs from the *II. SS-Panzerkorps* to the Soviets in two days, over 18,000 of these in a single day. The 11th US Armoured Division reported that the German POWs had been handed over to the Soviets for violating the surrender terms.

**15 MAY 1945**

On their first day as Soviet prisoners, *SS-Totenkopf* personnel were organised for rail transport to prison camps in Hungary and Romania. The transfer of *SS-Totenkopf* personnel to Soviet Union began in June/July 1945.

# APPENDIX 1

★ ★ ★

## COMMAND POSITIONS OF *I./SS-PANZER-REGIMENT 3*

**Abteilungskommandeure**

- *SS-Sturmbannführer* Leiner, 20 May 1942-21 October 1942 as commander of *SS-Panzer-Abteilung 4(III).*
- *SS-Hauptsturmführer* Meierdrees, 14 October 1942-20 August 1943, WIA (wounded in action).
- *SS-Hauptsturmführer* Säumenicht, 20 August 1943-20 January 1944.
- *SS-Sturmbannführer* Meierdrees, 20 January 1944-2 January 1945, KIA (killed in action).
- *SS-Obersturmführer* Lummitsch, 2 January 1945-20 January 1945.
- *SS-Hauptsturmführer* Anton Berlin, 20 January 1945-13 February 1945 (took command of *SS-Panzer-Regiment 3*).
- *SS-Hauptsturmführer* Alfons Martin, 13 February 1945-17 March 1945, KIA.
- *SS-Obersturmführer* Lummitsch, 17 March 1945-8 May 1945.

**Adjutanten**

- *SS-Obersturmführer* Altermüller, 1 July 1942-9 August 1943.
- *SS-Obersturmführer* Strobl, 11 August 1943-20 August 1943.
- *SS-Obersturmführer* Heckl, 20 August 1943-19 October 1943.
- *SS-Untersturmführer* Heise, 19 October 1943-15 February 1944.
- *SS-Obersturmführer* Strobl, 15 February 1944-30 April 1945 (transferred to *SS-Panzergrenadier-Regiment 6 'Eicke'*).
- *SS-Standarten Oberjunker* Dieter Baumann, 30 April 1945-8 May 1945.

**Ordonnanz-Offiziere**

- *SS-Hauptsturmführer* Dr Krogh-Christoffersen, 1 June 1942-23 February 1943.
- *SS-Untersturmführer* Herbatschek, 23 February 1943-11 August 1943.
- *SS-Untersturmführer* Borkmann, 11 August 1943-30 January 1944.
- *SS-Untersturmführer* Stege, 30 January 1944-30 July 1944, KIA.

- *SS-Untersturmführer* Steinegger, 30 July 1944-2 September 1944, WIA (KIA 5 January 1945).
- *SS-Untersturmführer* Connert, 2 September 1944-16 March 1945, KIA in Magyaralmás.
- *SS-Obersturmführer* Engelbrecht, 16 March 1945-8 May 1945 (transferred from *II./SS-Panzer-Regiment 3*).

**Nachrichten-Offiziere**

- *SS-Untersturmführer* Lux, 25 August 1942-15 November 1942 (transferred to *Stabskompanie* of *SS-Panzer-Regiment 3*).
- *SS-Untersturmführer* Korse, 15 November 1942-12 July 1943.
- *SS-Hauptscharführer* Quilitz, 12 July 1943-3 October 1943 (transferred to *7. Kompanie* of *SS-Panzer-Regiment 3* from 25 January 1943-1 March 1943 and was promoted to *SS-Untersturmführer der Reserve* on 9 November 1943 and *SS-Obersturmführer der Reserve* on 20 April 1944)
- *SS-Obersturmführer der Reserve* Quilitz 4 October 1943-2 January 1945, KIA in Dunaalmás.
- *SS-Unterscharführer* Kurt Arp, 2 January 1945-8 May 1945.

**IVa Offiziere**

- *SS-Untersturmführer* Wolf, 1 November 1942-7 May 1943
- *SS-Obersturmführer* Spieker, 7 May 1943-2 August 1944, KIA.
- *SS-Obersturmführer* Oeynhausen, 2 August 1944-21 November 1944 (transferred to *Stabskompanie* of *SS-Panzer-Regiment* ).

**IVb Offiziere**

- *SS-Hauptsturmführer* Dr Muhlich, 20 May 1942-5 November 1942 (transferred to regimental *Stab*).
- *SS-Obersturmführer* Reithmeyer, 5 November 1942-23 February 1943, WIA but died on 26 February 1943.
- *SS-Hauptsturmführer* Dr Krogh-Christoffersen, 23 February 1943-10 July 1943, WIA.
- *SS-Untersturmführer der Reserve* Dr Abt, 22 May 1944-1 March 1945 (transferred to *SS-San.-Ausb.u.Ers.Btl Stettin*).

**TFK (Technischer Führer für das Kraftfahrwesen)**

- *SS-Obersturmführer* Liersch, 10 April 1942-15 June 1942.
- *SS-Obersturmführer* Eisele, 15 June 1942-1 November 1942 (transferred to Regimental *Stab* as the new *TFK*).
- *SS-Hauptsturmführer* Klemme, 1 November 1942-30 January 1945.
- *SS-Untersturmführer* Reitwiessner, 30 January 1945-8 May 1945.

**TFW (Technischer Führer Waffenwesen)**

- *SS-Untersturmführer* Müller, 8 June 1942-1 November 1942.
- *SS-Obersturmführer* Kuhner, 10 June 1944-8 May 1945.

**Stabskompanie**

- *SS-Obersturmführer* Otto Friedrich, 1 July 1942-1 August 1942 (transferred to *7. Kompanie* of *II./SS-Panzer-Regiment 3*).
- *SS-Hauptsturmführer* Grams, 1 August 1942-4 October 1943.
- *SS-Obersturmführer* Nadel, 4 October 1943-18 January 1945 (took command of *Stabskompanie/SS-Panzer-Regiment 3*).

**Panzer-Pionierzug**

- *SS-Untersturmführer der Reserve* Mink, 1 March 1944-31 March 1945.

**Flak-Zug**

- *SS-Untersturmführer der Reserve* Vieweg, 15 December 1943-29 July 1944, WIA.
- *SS-Oberscharführer* Stoff till 8 May 1945.

**Panzer-Aufklärungszug**

- *SS-Untersturmführer* Quade, 1 July 1942-8 January 1943.
- *SS-Untersturmführer* Lummitsch, 8 January 1943-8 July 1943 (took command of *1. Kompanie*).
- *SS-Obersturmführer* Rudolph, 10 August 1944, KIA.
- *SS-Hauptscharführer* Dieter Baumann, 10 August 1944-30 April 1945.

**1./SS-Panzer-Regiment 3**

- *SS-Hauptsturmführer* Mooslechner, 1 June 1942 -6 December 1943 [took command of *4. (s) Kompanie (Tiger)*]
- *SS-Untersturmführer* Quarenghi, 6 December 1942-30 December 1942.
- *SS-Hauptsturmführer* Mooslechner, 30 December 1942-20 February 1943.
- *SS-Obersturmführer* Riefkogel, 20 February 1943-8 July 1943, WIA (transferred from *II./SS-Panzer-Regiment 3*).
- *SS-Untersturmführer* Lummitsch, 8 July 1943-13 July 1943, WIA.
- *SS-Obersturmführer* Altermüller, 13 July 1943-11 August 1943 (*1.* and *2. Kompanien* were merged to form a single *Kampfgruppe* on 9 August 1943. The first commander of the *Kampfgruppe* was *SS-Obersturmführer* Burgschulte, KIA 11 August 1943).
- *SS-Obersturmführer* Riefkogel, WIA 11 August 1943.
- *SS-Hauptsturmführer* Säumenicht, 11 August 1943-20 August 1943.

- *SS-Untersturmführer* von Rennenkampf, 21 August 1943-25 December 1943.
- *SS-Hauptsturmführer* Riefkogel, 25 December 1943-28 July 1944, KIA.
- *SS-Obersturmführer* Schramm, 28 July 1944-19 September 1944, KIA.
- *SS-Obersturmführer* Herbatschek, 19 September 1944-21 September 1944 (*1.* and *3. Kompanien* under the command of *SS-Obersturmführer* Herbatschek, known as *Kampfgruppe Herbatschek*).
- *SS-Hauptsturmführer* Balzer, 21 September 1944-16 December 1944 (merged with *2. Kompanie* to form *Kampfgruppe Balzer*, *SS-Hauptsturmführer* Balzer assumed temporary command of *SS-Panzer-Regiment 3* on 26 January 1945).
- *SS-Untersturmführer* Müller, 26 January 1945-28 January 1945 KIA during a bombing raid on Gárdony.
- *SS-Obersturmführer* Lummitsch, 28 January 1945 (took command of the remaining elements of *1., 2., 3.* and *4. Kompanien* and formed *Kampfgruppe Lummitsch;* after *SS-Hauptsturmführer* Martin was killed on 17 March 1945, *SS-Obersturmführer* Lummitsch took command of the remnants of the *Abteilung*).

**2./SS-Panzer-Regiment 3**

- *SS-Obersturmführer* Kanth, 1 June 1942-15 November 1942 (assumed command of the new *Tiger-Kompanie*).
- *SS-Obersturmführer* Flohr, 15 November 1942-12 July 1943, KIA 30 July 1943 (while leading *5. Kompanie*).
- *SS-Obersturmführer* Burgschulte, 12 July 1943-11 August 1943, KIA (*2. Kompanie* merged with *1. Kompanie* on 9 August 1943).
- *SS-Hauptsturmführer* Säumenicht, 11 August 1943-20 August 1943 (assumed command of *I./SS-Panzer-Regiment 3* after *SS-Hauptsturmführer* Meierdrees had been wounded; transferred on 5 May 1944 *SS-Hauptsturmführer* Säumenicht to *SS-Panzer-Regiment 5* and assumed command of *I./SS-Panzer-Regiment 5* on 19 May 1944).
- *SS-Hauptsturmführer* Säumenicht, 20 January 1944-5 February 1944.
- *SS-Hauptsturmführer* Bormuth, 5 February 1944-10 July 1944 (transferred to *SS-Panzer-Regiment 12* and took command of *1. Kompanie*).
- *SS-Hauptsturmführer* Balzer, 10 July 1944-21 September 1944 (took command of *1. Kompanie* which merged with *2. Kompanie* to form *Kampfgruppe* Balzer as described above).
- *SS-Obersturmführer der Reserve* Linsenmayer, 16 December 1944-28 January 1945 (*2. Kompanie* was merged with *Kampfgruppe Lummitsch* on 28 January 1945).

**3./SS-Panzer-Regiment 3**

- *SS-Hauptsturmführer* Gross, 1 June 1942-15 November 1942 (transferred to *SS-Panzer-Regiment 1*).

- *SS-Obersturmführer* Nerpel, 15 November 1942-9 August 1943 (transferred to *5. Kompanie of II./SS-Panzer-Regiment 3.*) KIA 11 August 1943.
- *SS-Obersturmführer* Altermüller, 9 August 1943-11 August 1943, KIA 11 August 1943.

On 9 August 1943, *3.* and *4. Kompanien* were merged to form the second *Abteilung Kampfgruppe*. The first commander was *SS-Obersturmführer* Altermüller, KIA 11 August 1943. After *SS-Obersturmführer* Altermüller was killed both *Kampfgruppen* were combined into a single *Kampfgruppe*. The commanders of this *Kampfgruppe* were:

- *SS-Obersturmführer* Herbatschek, 11 August 1943-20 August 1943, WIA.
- *SS-Obersturmführer* Strobl, 20 August 1943-4 October 1943 (later transferred to SS-Pz.Gr.Ausb.u.Ers.Btl 3 until the 15 February 1944).
- *SS-Hauptsturmführer* Zech, 1 November 1943-30 July 1944, WIA.
- *SS-Obersturmführer* Herbatschek, 30 July 1944-28 August 1944 (from 28 August 1944-1 September 1944 *Kampfgruppe Herbatschek* was formed with *4. Kompanie* temporarily placed under the command of *SS-Obersturmführer* Herbatschek).
- *SS-Obersturmführer* Herbatschek, 1 September 1944-18 September 1944 (from 19 September 1944-21 September 1944, *Kampfgruppe Herbatschek* was established with the attachment of *1. Kompanie* to *3. Kompanie*).
- *SS-Obersturmführer* Herbatschek, 21 September 1944-28 January 1945 (*3. Kompanie* integrated into *Kampfgruppe Lummitsch* on 28 January 1945).

### *4. (schwere) Tiger /SS-Panzer-Regiment 3 (Feldpost Nummer 48786)*

- *SS-Obersturmführer* Kanth, 15 November 1942-20 February 1942 (transferred to the *Stabskompanie* of *SS-Panzer-Regiment 3* on 20 February 1943).
- *SS-Obersturmführer* Mooslechner, 20 February 1942-19 March 1943, KIA near Iwanowka.
- *SS-Hauptsturmführer* Biermeier, 19 March 1943-9 May 1943 (*SS-Hauptsturmführer* Biermeier assumed command of *II./SS-Panzer-Regiment 3*).
- On 9 May 1943, the *4 (schwere) Kompanie* was renamed *9. Kompanie* of *II./SS-Panzer-Regiment 3.*

### 4./SS-Panzer-Regiment 3

- A new *4. Kompanie* was formed 9 May 1943 with *Feldpost Nummer 57182* issued on 15 February 1943 and placed under the command of *SS-Obersturmführer* Eckl.
- *SS-Obersturmführer* Eckl, 9 May 1943-28 July 1943 (Eckl had served with *SS-Panzer-Abteilung 4 (III)* and *I./SS-Panzer-Regiment 3* from 20 June 1942

as a *Zugführer*. After being wounded Eckl was transferred to the *SS-Panzer-Ausbildungs- und Ersatz-Regiment Bitsch* on 13 September 1943; he was posted to the *SS-FHA, In 6, Amt IIa*).

- On 9 August 1943, *4. Kompanie* was amalgamated with *3. Kompanie.*
- *SS-Untersturmführer* von Kleist, 28 July 1943-9 August 1943.

*4. Kompanie* was reformed in Grafenwöhr and issued a new *Feldpost Nummer (48182)* on 4 October 1943.

- *SS-Obersturmführer* Lummitsch, 19 December 1943-26 July 1944, WIA Lummitsch and evacuated 27 July 1944.
- *SS-Obersturmführer* Retzdorf, 26 July 1944-30 July 1944, KIA in Siedlce.
- *SS-Obersturmführer* von Kleist, 30 July 1944-28 August 1944, WIA.
- *SS-Obersturmführer* Herbatschek, 28 August 1944-1 September 1944 (*Kampfgruppe Herbatschek* with *3.* and *4. Kompanien* combined into a single *Kampfgruppe*).
- *SS-Obersturmführer* Lummitsch, 1 September 1944-2 January 1945.
- *SS-Scharführer* Jensen, 2 January 1945-20 January 1945 (at the time, *SS-Scharführer* Jensen had been serving as the *Kompanie-Spiess*).
- *SS-Obersturmführer* Lummitsch, 20 January 1945-28 January 1945. ( *SS-Obersturmführer* Lummitsch formed *Kampfgruppe Lummitsch* on 28 January 1945 which integrated *1., 2., 3.* and *4. Kompanien* into a single *Kampfgruppe; the Spiess for this Kampfgruppe was SS-Hauptscharführer Pehl; SS-Obersturmführer* Lummitsch was also temporarily commander of *I./SS-Panzer-Regiment 3* from 2 January 1945 to 20 January 1945).

**Leichte Kolonne**

- *SS-Untersturmführer* Holler, 1 January 1943-25 March 1944 ( transferred to *III./SS-Panzer-Artillerie-Regiment 3* in May 1944).

**Versorgungs-Kompanie**

- *SS-Hauptsturmführer* Geiling, 25 March 1944-25 July 1944.

Upon arrival in Warsaw, the *Versorgungs-Kompanie* was put under direct control of the *Panzer-Regiment*. The *I./SS-Panzer-Regiment 3* had to organize a new *Versorgungs-Kompanie* from existing vehicle stocks and placed *SS-Untersturmführer* Kaden in command.

- *SS-Untersturmführer* Kaden, 25 July 1944-17 April 1945 (transferred to *1. SS-Panzer-Division 'Leibstandarte'*).
- *SS-Oberscharführer* Wunsch, 17 April 1945-8 May 1945.

# APPENDIX 2

★ ★ ★

## Knight's Cross Recipients of *I./SS-Panzer-Regiment 3*

Citation reports for the Knight,s Cross awards for *SS-Hauptsturmführer* Riefkogel, *SS-Hauptsturmführer* Säumenicht, the Oak Leaves of the Knight,s Cross to *SS-Hauptsturmführer* Meierdrees and German Cross in Gold to *SS-Untersturmführer* Lummitsch.

On 30 March 1943, ***SS-Obersturmführer*** **Riefkogel** was nominated for the Knight's Cross of the Iron Cross for his actions during the night of 16/17 March 1943, his citation reads as follows:

*Citation for SS-Obersturmführer Waldemar Riefkogel*
*Born 7 January 1913*
*Knight's Cross on 11 July 1943*

*SS-Pz.Gr.Div. 'Totenkopf on 30 March 1943*

*Short Comments on the Justification for the Award by Superior Commanders*

*With the defences struggling to hold Tschugujew (Chuhuiv/Chuguev) after it was captured,* SS-Obersturmführer *Riefkogel with his* Panzer-Kompanie *helped* I./SS-Panzergrenadier-Regiment 'Totenkopf' *during the night of 16/17 March 1943. The Russians launched a strong counterattack with mounted infantry and tank support. The Russians hoped to retake the town after achieving a breakthrough.*

SS-Obersturmführer *Riefkogel with his* Kompanie, *which consisted of two operational Panzers without infantry support, advanced towards the attacking enemy which by this time had forced a breakthrough of our front line,* SS-Obersturmführer *Riefkogel knocked out two Russian tanks and forced the enemy infantry to abandon their positions. Almost immediately the Russians regrouped and launched another attack, but again due to the heroic actions of* SS-Obersturmführer *Riefkogel this attack also failed.*

*Some hours later in the sector of* 3 Kompanie *the Russians made a strong attack with truck-mounted infantry and tank support against our positions. At the time* SS-Obersturmführer *Riefkogel was assisting in the recovery of damaged Panzers and by his own decision immediately joined his two operational Panzers to launch a counterattack during which he knocked out four T-34 tanks. He also noticed that the Russians were trying to outflank the positions held by* 3. Kompanie *whereupon he ordered his crew to bail out of the Panzer and at the head of his men led an infantry assault into the attacking Russians which came as a shock to the Russians. With his immediate intervention,* SS-Obersturmführer *Riefkogel broke the Russian assault despite being wounded twice by shell fragments.* SS-Obersturmführer *Riefkogel did not leave his men. Due to his bold, heroic action he prevented the Russians from re-capturing Tschugujew (Chuhuiv/Chuguev).*

*I request that* SS-Obersturmführer *Riefkogel be recommended for the Knight's Cross of the Iron Cross in recognition of his heroic success and bravery.*

*Signed, Simon*

*Divisional Commander,* SS-Brigadeführer und Generalmajor der Waffen-SS

*Submitted to the Führerhauptquartier 9 July 1943*

*Endorsed by Generalleutant Schmundt*

Citation for the Knight's Cross of the Iron Cross for ***SS-Hauptsturmführer*** Säumenicht.

SS-Hauptsturmführer *Rudolf Säumenicht*
*Born 13 February 1916*
*Knight's Cross on 13 October 1943*

*Proposal Nr 2220, for the awarding of Knight's Cross of the Iron Cross*

*Awarded on 13 October 1943 from the Headquarters OKH, 11 October 1943*

*Short Notice on the Justification and Acceptance by Superior Commanders*

*During the morning hours on 2 September 1943 the Russians carried out a strong artillery and mortar strike which supported a large attack on the division's left flank which was carried out with tanks and infantry. This attack was executed with two rifle divisions and about 130 tanks reinforced with ground-attack aircraft support. The enemy managed to breach our front lines but during this difficult moment* SS-Hauptsturmführer Säumenicht, *with his* Panzer-Kampfgruppe *which consisted of one Panzer VI, five Pz IV's and six Panzer III's, by his own decision decided to launch a counterattack against the Russian forces.*

*The Russian* forces *were supported by strong artillery fire during the attack and in fierce fighting* SS-Hauptsturmführer Säumenicht and his Kampfgruppe *attacked the enemy in the flank of their massed infantry formations which took them by surprise and forced them back. During the day's action,* SS-Hauptsturmführer Säumenicht's Kampfgruppe *destroyed at total of 42 T-34 tanks.* SS-Hauptsturmführer Säumenicht and his men were an example of bravery and readiness *and through his concise orders his* Kampfgruppe *only lost two Panzers. The Russian leadership had hoped for a breakthrough at this crucial spot by using the 6th Rifle Division. This information was determined by radio intercepts and information gleaned from prisoners.*

SS-Hauptsturmführer Säumenicht inflicted the heaviest losses on the enemy by his decisive leadership and prudent action which prevented a Russian breakthrough. I request that SS-Hauptsturmführer Säumenicht be awarded the Knight*'s Cross of the Iron Cross*

*Divisional Commander, Priess*

SS-Brigadeführer und Generalmajor der Waffen-SS

Citation for the Oak Leaves to Knight's Cross of the Iron Cross for ***SS-Hauptsturmführer*** **Meierdrees** read as follows:

SS-Hauptsturmführer *Erwin Meierdrees*
Abteilungskommandeur of I./SS-Panzer-Regiment 3
*Born 11 December 1916 in Wesel*

*During the attack on Uljanowka on 1 March 1943, our advancing Panzers were stopped by a strong Russian anti-tank gun front.* SS-Hauptsturmführer *Meierdrees using his own Panzer made a bold attack against the flank of the anti-tank gun front and thus allowed the advance to continue.*

*In the early morning hours of the 3 March 1943, the Panzers of Meierdrees unit were in the area of Schljachowaja where they surprised a Russian motorised column about 7 km long which consisted of artillery and anti-tank guns. Using his own initiative he immediately moved forward with his own men. The speed of the attack by the* Abteilung *on the Russian column was a complete success. Several artillery and 40 anti-tank guns along with several hundred vehicles were destroyed. The Russian column was escorted by 15 T-34 tanks which were also destroyed.*

*On 7 July 1943, the expected Russian attack along the Radin-Schopino road was launched with the support of infantry and tanks. This attacking force was engaged by* SS-Hauptsturmführer *Meierdrees and his Abteilung, which at this time did not have any infantry support. His forward* Kompanie *observed a strong Russian infantry concentration in Regimental strength about 1.5 km east of the* Abteilung *which was at the time positioned in a ravine. With only a light* Kompanie *(Panzer IIIs),* SS-Hauptsturmführer *Meierdrees attacked this enemy concentration causing heavy losses to the enemy who then retreated. He then led the medium* Kompanie *(Panzer IVs) against a Russian tank force which resulted in five Russian tanks being destroyed in the shortest possible time. By his resolute leadership* SS-Hauptsturmführer *Meierdrees prevented the blocking of the main road.*

*In the attack and defence of the Psel Bridgehead,* SS-Hauptsturmführer *Meierdrees and his* Panzer-Abteilung *were in constant action. During the attack on the barracks in Kljutschi on 12 July 1943, his* Abteilung *came across a complex Russian trench system which was defended by Russian infantry supported by tanks. As his* Panzer-Abteilung *approached the enemy the Russian tanks withdrew but the Russian infantry attacked the* Panzer-Abteilung, *causing several of our Panzers to be damaged.* SS-Hauptsturmführer *Meierdrees' own Panzer was hit and immobilised and along with his crew and gathering other crews from damaged Panzers carried the fight to the enemy in the infantry role.*

*During the battle for Hill 213.9 on the Mius, the* Abteilung *of* SS-Hauptsturmführer *Meierdrees was the first to engage the enemy. With fortitude he led the* Panzer-Abteilung *from the front against the enemy while coming under the most intense artillery and anti-tank gunfire.*

*During the battle, Meierdrees' Panzer was knocked out and he, along with his crew, had to bail out, from there he carried the fight to the enemy in the infantry role. On 1 August 1943, when for the fifth time the* Abteilung *dashed forward under strong enemy artillery fire, his* Abteilung *managed to seize and occupy the height. His* Abteilung *repelled all enemy counterattacks which consisted of infantry and tanks.*

*During the establishment of the bridgehead Kolontajew between 19 August 1943 and 20 August 1943,* SS-Hauptsturmführer *Meierdrees and his* Abteilung *distinguished themselves yet again. Regardless of the strong enemy artillery and anti-tank gunfire he advanced along with his* Abteilung *to the north-east and took Hill 167.5 and held his position despite intense enemy pressure. During the battle* SS-Hauptsturmführer *Meierdrees was wounded for the fifth time.*

*Signed, Priess*

*Divisional Commander,* SS-Brigadeführer und Generalmajor der Waffen-SS

It should be noted that the last Knight's Cross for *I./SS-Panzer-Regiment 3* was awarded to *SS-Obersturmführer* Lummitsch on 5 May 1945 and presented to him by the divisional commander, *SS-Brigadeführer* Becker. The award of the Knight's Cross to *SS-Obersturmführer* Lummitsch had been approved by the commander of the *6. Panzerarmee, SS-Oberstgruppenführer* Dietrich.

**_SS-Obersturmführer_ Rudolf Lummitsch Assessment report 1944**

*Military Unit and Service Branch: I./SS-Panzer-Regiment 3*
*Dated 26 August 1944*

*Subject: Promotion within the Waffen-SS*

*Attachments: reports concerning promotion to* SS-Untersturmführer
*1. Handwritten biography.*
*2. Personal details.*
*3. SS Number.*
*4. Two photographs.*

*To SS-FHA Amt V/IIa Berlin-Wilmersdorf*

*That* SS-Obersturmführer *Lummitsch, active Res SS-Nr 318-946, be recommended for promotion to* SS-Haupsturmführer der Reserve *of the* Waffen-SS.

*Birthday: 26 October 1920*
*Current position:* Kompanie-Chef, *appointed 19 December 1943*
*Last promotion: 20 April 1943, RDA*
*After being appointed as an officer within the* Waffen-SS, *he served as* Zugführer

*Courses*

1. *Kriegs Junker Lehrgang at Braunschweig 28 January 1940 to 10 May 1940.*
2. *Lehrgang für Heeres-Panzer-Aufklärungs-Schule at Potsdam-Krampnitz 1 March 1941 to 15 April 1941.*
3. *Kompanieführer-Lehrgang at Erlangen and Putlos 7 February 1944 to 17 February 1944.*

*The proposal for promotion is based on abilities demonstrated while serving as a* Kompanie-Chef *during the refurbishment and operational phases following March 1944.*

*Assessment of Character, Fitness, Duty, Instructional Ability and SS Attitude*

*Lummitsch has served within* I. Abteilung *as* Chef *of* 4. Kompanie. *His character is open and honest. He displays an excellent attitude while on and off duty. In combat he has fully proven himself, he has always performed without consideration to his personal safety and the positions entrusted to him as a* Kompanie-Chef *have been conducted with prudence and personal bravery; as a well-motIVated* SS-Mann, *he his imbued with the right political attitude.*

*Campaigns and Operational Theatres:*

- Russian Campaign SS-T Division 1941-October 1942.
- Russian Campaign SS-T Pz.Gren.Div. Feb 1943- August 1943.
- Russian Campaign SS-T Pz. Div. 25 July 1944-27 July 1944.

*Awards*

- Iron Cross, First Class
- Iron Cross, Second Class
- German Cross in Gold
- Wound Badge, in Silver and Bronze
- Tank Assault Badge, in Silver and Bronze

*Current Proposal: as* Kompanie-Chef
*Date of Marriage: 19 February 1944*
*Birthday of Spouse: 28 June February2*
*Number of Children: None*
*Birthday of first Child: None*
*Entry into the SS: 15 January 1938*
*Faith/Denomination: a believer in God*
*Suitable grade: KV*

*Signed,* SS-Sturmbannführer *Meierdrees*
Abteilungsführer

*Comments of Superior Commanding Officer*
*Promotion is approved.*
*Signed,* SS-Sturmbannführer *and Regimental Commanding Officer, Laackmann*

*Comments by the Divisional Commanding Officer*
*The preferred promotion of this highly valued and excellent officer who is currently serving as a* Kompanie-Chef *cannot be justified or endorsed because of his age; he is too young to hold such a rank. His personal bravery cannot be disputed or is beyond doubt, but my decision is final.*

*Divisional Command Post, 5 September 1944*
*Signed, Divisional Commanding Officer,* SS-Oberführer *Becker*

**Award for German Cross in Gold to *SS-Untersturmführer* Lummitsch**

*Proposal Number 39; Award of the German Cross in Gold*

*Regimental Command Post, 6 August 1943*
*Commanding Officer, SS-Sturmbannführer Bochmann*

*To OKH/Pz I.Staffel V e.d.D*

*Name: Rudolf Lummitsch*
*Date of Birth: 26 October 1920 in Konnern in Saale*
*Rank and Service:* SS-Obersturmführer *(active)*
*Troop and Unit: SS-Pz.Rgt. 3,* Stabskompanie I. Abt.
*Awards:*
*Wound Badge Bronze: 6 July 1941.*
*Iron Cross, second class: 9 July 1941.*
*Iron Cross, first class: 16 August 1941.*
*Wound Badge, Silver: 17 August 1941.*
*Tank Assault Badge, Bronze: 14 October 1941.*
*Eastern Medal: 25 July 1942.*

*Operational Theatres since 1939:*
*Polish Campaign (gunner).*
*Western Campaign (as platoon leader).*
*Eastern Campaign (leader of Panzerspähwagen, Kompanie and platoon leader with the* Aufklärungs-Abteilung*).*
*With the* Panzer-Regiment; Panzer-Zugführer *of the regimental* Aufklärungszug

*I./SS-Pz.Rgt. 3* Panzer-Aufklärungszug *and* Kompanie-Chef.

Proposal for the Knight's Cross

Reasons and Opinions for the Award by his Superiors

*During the attack on Korowitschino on 4 October 1942,* SS-Obersturmführer *Lummitsch as a leader of a reinforced* Panzerspähzug *demonstrated heroic bravery. Without hesitation he drove forward with his* Wagen *during which he was hit whilst in the lead, with his crew he continued the attack on foot where he destroyed seven Russian bunkers and four ant-tank rifles. Even though he was wounded he still continued to attack, mounting a third* Panzerspähwagen, *until Korowitschino was captured, only then did Lummitsch seek medical attention from the medical officer.*

*On 5 October 1942, SS-Obersturmführer Lummitsch and his was ordered to advance eastwards with his* Panzerspähwagen-Zug *in the direction of Ssutokij to repel a Russian assault on the so-called 'Roundhead Position' and destroy the Russian force. Immediately upon emerging he came under heavy Russian fire which nearly stalled our counterattack, but with his* Zug, SS-Obersturmführer *Lummitsch drove forward and pressed home the attack which resulted in the destruction of four anti-tank rifles and two heavy machine guns. Further to this, following the attack, Lummitsch also managed to capture 44 POWs, 11 machine guns, 80 rifles and a further six anti-tank rifles.*

*On 23 February 1943, as a leader of a* Panzerzug *advancing on Kotschereshki-Wjasowak in a wedge formation, he was attacked from the flank. He immediately launched a decisive counterattack which destroyed seven (7.62cm) anti-tank guns.*

*During the attack on Kljutschi on 12 July 1943,* SS-Obersturmführer *Lummitsch excelled himself by displaying courage and bravery while leading* 1. Kompanie. *During the attack he rolled over a* Pak-Front *during an attack on a barracks where his tank was knocked out. Lummitsch and his crew bailed out. Despite being wounded for a fifth time, he continued to attack the Russian positions in the infantry role during which he created the opportunity for the capture of the barracks by our infantry forces.*

*Signed,* SS-Sturmbannführer *and Regimental Commander Bochmann*

*SS-Pz.Gren.Div 'Totenkopf',* Divisional Command Post, *9 August 1943*

*The proposal for award of the German Cross in Gold to SS-Obersturmführer Lummitsch is endorsed by me.* SS-Obersturmführer *Lummitsch is a young, dashing and extremely brave officer who displayed a state of readiness despite his wounds.*

*Signed,* SS-Brigadführer und Generalmajor der Waffen-SS *Priess*

*Supplemental II SS-Pz Korps*
*Endorsed*
*Signed, Hausser*

*Supplemental Report by SS-Pz.Gren.Div 'Totenkopf'*

SS-Untersturmführer *Lummitsch who has fought in the east since the first days has always displayed a constant readiness and has over and over again displayed extraordinary bravery while serving with the 'Totenkopf' Division and has been wounded four times. I ask that* SS-Untersturmführer *Lummitsch, who has proven his bravery, be award the German Cross in Gold.*

Divisionsführer und Generalmajor der Waffen-SS *Priess*

*Opinion of II. SS-Pz.Korps*
*The proposal of the award to* SS-Untersturmführer *Lummitsch is endorsed.*

*Signed, Hausser*

*F.d.R.d.a*
SS-Hauptsturmführer *and* Korpsadjutant

# APPENDIX 3

★ ★ ★

## OFFICERS FROM *I./SS-PANZER-REGIMENT 3* KILLED IN THE LINE OF DUTY

- *SS-Untersturmführer* der Reserve **Dr Abt**, IVb KIA 3 April 1945.
- *SS-Untersturmführer* **Mittag, Werner** KIA 30 April 1945.
- *SS-Obersturmführer* **Dr Reithmeyer**, IVb KIA 26 February 1943.
- *SS-Hauptsturmführer* **Mooslechner**, KIA 19 March 1943, *Chef* of *4. (schwere) Kompanie.*
- *SS-Untersturmführer* **Ratajczek**, KIA 12 July 1943, *Zugführer* of *2. Kompanie.*
- *SS-Untersturmführer* **Moosbrucker**, KIA 30 July 1943, *Zugführer* of *1. Kompanie.*
- *SS-Untersturmführer* **Granzeuer**, KIA 30 July 1943, *Zugführer* of *1. Kompanie.*
- *SS-Untersturmführer* **Hortsmann**, KIA 30 July 1943, *Stabskompanie* (commanded the *Kradmelderzug*).
- *SS-Hauptsturmführer* **Flohr**, KIA 30 July 1943 as *Chef* of *5. Kompanie* (former *2. Kompanie Chef* until 12 July 1943).
- *SS-Obersturmführer* **Altermüller**, KIA 10 August 1943, *Chef* of *4. Kompanie.*
- *SS-Hauptsturmführer* **Nerpal**, KIA 11 August 1943 as *Chef* of *5. Kompanie* but had led *3. Kompanie* until 9 August 1943.
- *SS-Obersturmführer* **Burgschulte**, KIA 11 August 1943, *Chef* of *2. Kompanie* (transferred from 1st *Zug* of *5. Kompanie*).
- *SS-Untersturmführer* **Quade**, KIA 30 August 1943, *9. Kompanie* (former *Führer* of *Panzer-Aufklärungszug* of *Stabskompanie* from *I./SS-Panzer-Regiment 3*).
- *SS-Untersturmführer* **Quarenghi**, died 5 November 1943, *Zugführer* of *1. Kompanie.*
- *SS-Obersturmführer* **Heise**, KIA 26 July 1944, *Zugführer* of *2. Kompanie.*
- *SS-Hauptsturmführer* **Riefkogel**, died 30 July 1944, WIA 28 July 1944, *Chef* of *1. Kompanie.*
- *SS-Obersturmführer* **Retzdorf**, KIA 30 July 1944, *Chef* of *4. Kompanie.*

- *SS-Untersturmführer* **Stege**, KIA 30 July 1944, *Ordonnanz-Offizier* of *I./SS-Panzer-Regimemt 3.*
- *SS-Hauptsturmführer* **Spieker**, KIA 2 August 1944, *IVa* of *I./SS-Panzer-Regiment 3.*
- *SS-Obersturmführer* **Rudolph**, KIA 10 August 1944, *Führer* of the *Panzer-Aufklärungszug.*
- *SS-Obersturmführer* **Schramm**, KIA 18 September 1944, *Chef* of *1. Kompanie.*
- *SS-Sturmbannführer* **Meierdrees**, KIA 2 January 1945, *Abteilungskommandeur.*
- *SS-Obersturmführer* **Qualitz**, KIA 2 January 1945, *Nachrichten-Offizier* of *I./SS-Panzer-Regiment 3.*
- *SS-Untersturmführer der Reserve* **Steinegger**, KIA 5 January 1945, *Ordonnanz-Offizier* of *I./SS-Panzer Regiment 3.*
- *SS-Untersturmführer* **Müller**, KIA 28 January 1945, *Chef* of *1. Kompanie.*
- *SS-Untersturmführer* C**onnert**, KIA 16 March 1945, *Ordonnanz-Offizier* of *I./SS-Panzer-Regiment 3.*
- *SS-Hauptsturmführer* **Martin**, KIA 17 March 1945, as *Abteilungskommandeur.*
- *SS-Obersturmführer* **von Kliest**, KIA 6 April 1945, former *Chef* of *4. Kompanie* (died while attached to *Panzer-Brigade* 'Westfalen').
- *SS-Untersturmführer* **Ober**, KIA 7 April 1945, *I./SS-Panzer-Regiment 3.*

Note: *SS-Untersturmführer* Connert was killed by artillery fire in Magyaralmás while trying to reach cover near the *Abteilung* command post.

# APPENDIX 4

★ ★ ★

## Pz. V Panther, Bergepanther and SPW issues for *I./SS-Panzer-Regiment 3*

### Sd.Kfz. 171 Panther

| Stock | Allocation date | Sent on | Zug nr. | Remarks |
|---|---|---|---|---|
| 4 | 23 December 1943 | 1 January 1944 | 6440872 | Arrived on 13 January 1944 |
| 6 | 27 February 1944 | 3 March 1944 | | |
| 5 | 16 May 1944 | 8 June 1944 | 755 | Arrived on 18 June 1944 |
| 8 | 24 June 1944 | 11 July 1944 | 6581304 | |
| 2 | 24 June 1944 | 17 July 1944 | | No personnel |
| 2 | 20 June 1944 | 12 July 1944 | 6584355 | Handed over from *I./ Panzer-Regiment 27* |
| 1 | 20 June 1944 | 14 July 1944 | 6584355 | Handed over from *I./ Panzer-Regiment 27* |
| 8 | 3 July 1944 | 11 July 1944 | | |
| 8 | 3 July 1944 | 14 July 1944 | 6584599 | |
| 8 | 3 July 1944 | 14 July 1944 | 6584600 | |
| 8 | 3 July 1944 | 15 July 1944 | 6584623 | |
| 8 | 3 July 1944 | 16 July 1944 | 6584624 | |
| 8 | 3 July 1944 | 14 July 1944 | | |
| 5 | 3 July 1944 | 17 July 1944 | 6584680 | Exchanged, these Panthers re-issued to *I./Panzer-Regiment 16* |
| 5 | 3 July 1944 | 17 July 1944 | 6584681 | Befehlspanthers |
| 2 | 20 July 1944 | 21 July 1944 | | |
| 4 | 20 July 1944 | 25 July 1944 | 1045 | Handed over from *I./ Panzer-Regiment 27* |

**Notes:**

Five Panthers handed over to *SS-Panzer-Regiment 1* by order of *Generalinspekteur der Panzertruppen*, on 30 April 1944. The Panthers were collected at Mailly-le-Camp on 12 May 1944.

The last four Panthers issued on 25 July 1944 were sent by rail on 26 July 1944, and arrived on 31 July 1944 in *Bahnhof* Lochow.

The Panthers issued in June and July 1944 were issued from *Heereszeugamt* Breslau and *Heereszeugamt* Magdeburg.

### Bergepanthers

| Stock | Allocation date | Sent on | Zug nr. | Remarks |
|---|---|---|---|---|
| 2 | | 30 April 1944 | | Arrived on 8 June 1944, issued to *Panzer-Werkstattzug* of *I./SS-Panzer-Regiment 3* |
| 2 | 13 September 1944 | 4 October 1944 | 1352 | Arrived on 9 November 1944, issued to *Panzer-Werkstatt-Kompanie of SS-Panzer-Regiment 3* |
| 2 | 28 October 1944 | 15 November 1944 | 1495 | Arrived on 24 November 1944, issued to *Panzer-Werkstatt-Kompanie of SS-Panzer-Regiment 3* |

### SPW

| Stock | Allocation date | Sent on | Zug nr. | Remarks |
|---|---|---|---|---|
| 5 | 21 July 1944 | n/a | n/a | |

# APPENDIX 5

★ ★ ★

## Operational Status 1944-1945

**Operational/Short -term repair/Long-term repair**

| Date | Status | Remarks |
|---|---|---|
| 29.02.1944 | - / - / - | |
| 23.03.1944 | 10 / - / - | |
| 25.03.1944 | 10 / - / - | |
| 01.04.1944 | | In transit |
| 20.04.1944 | 7 / 3 / - | |
| 01.05.1944 | 4 / 1 / - | |
| 15.05.1944 | 4 / 1 / - | |
| 01.06.1944 | 3 / 2 / - | |
| 10.06.1944 | ? / ? / ? | Six Panthers on strength |
| 01.07.1944 | 6 / 4 / - | |
| 24.07.1944 | 7 / ? / ? | |
| 25.07.1944 | 10 / - / - | 10 Panthers at 06.35 hours, at 07.25 hours five Panthers, at 12.00 hours six Panthers, at 15.30 hours 42 Panthers. |
| 26.07.1944 | 35 / ? / ? | At 06.50 hours 35 Panthers, at 10.30 hours 37 Panthers, (20 Panthers with *VIII. A.K*). During the relief attacks around Mordy, the Soviets report 60 Panthers being involved. |
| 27.07.1944 | 4 / ? / ? | Four Panthers reported during the morning, at 14.35 hours only three Panthers are reported operational. |
| 28.07.1944 | 8 / ? / ? | Four Panthers at 22.15 hours (in short term repairs six Panthers). With *Kampfgruppe Meierdrees* two *Befehlspanthers* and 23 Panthers. |
| 29.07.1944 | 14 / ? / ? | |

| Date | Status | Remarks |
|---|---|---|
| 30.07.1944 | 14 / ? / ? | 18 other Panthers reported operational at the western exit of Siedlce during the afternoon |
| 31.07.1944 | 18 / 23 / 6 | The *1. Kompanie* with 10 Panthers attached to *III./SS-Panzergrenadier-Regiment 5 'Totenkopf'* |
| 01.08.1944 | 22 / 30 / 5 | |
| 02.08.1944 | 18 / ? / ? | Later 19 Panthers are reported operational |
| 03.08.1944 | 8 / ? / ? | Later 21 Panthers are reported operational |
| 04.08.1944 | 24 / 25 / 8 | |
| 05.08.1944 | 28 / 18 / 6 | |
| 06.08.1944 | 32 / ? / ? | |
| 07.08.1944 | 32 / ? / ? | |
| 08.08.1944 | 34 / ? / ? | |
| 09.08.1944 | 36 / 15 / 2 | |
| 10.08.1944 | 34 / 18 / 2 | |
| 11.08.1944 | 33 / 20 / 2 | |
| 12.08.1944 | 30 / 23 / 2 | 33 Panthers reported later |
| 13.08.1944 | 24 / 30 / 3 | |
| 14.08.1944 | 30 / 24 / 3 | Also 24 Panthers reported later |
| 15.08.1944 | 32 / 22 / 3 | |
| 16.08.1944 | 33 / 21 / 3 | |
| 17.08.1944 | 40 / 14 / 3 | |
| 18.08.1944 | 40 / ? / ? | |
| 19.08.1944 | 44 / ? / ? | |
| 20.08.1944 | 36 / ? / ? | 44 Panthers reported later |

| Date | Status | Remarks |
|---|---|---|
| 21.08.1944 | 33 / ? / ? | |
| 23.08.1944 | 32 / ? / ? | |
| 24.08.1944 | 32 / ? / ? | |
| 25.08.1944 | 32 / ? / ? | |
| 26.08.1944 | 33 / ? / ? | |
| 27.08.1944 | 27 / ? / ? | Three Panthers from *1. Kompanie*, attached to *5. SS-Panzer-Division 'Wiking'* until 1 September 1944, also 33 Panthers reported later |
| 29.08.1944 | 23 / ? / ? | |
| 30.08.1944 | 21 / ? / ? | |
| 31.08.1944 | 26 / ? / ? | |
| 01.09.1944 | 20 / 8 / 22 | |
| 02.09.1944 | 26 / ? / ? | |
| 03.09.1944 | 31 / ? / ? | |
| 04.09.1944 | 24 / ? / ? | |
| 06.09.1944 | 25 / ? / ? | |
| 07.09.1944 | 23 / ? / ? | |
| 09.09.1944 | 27 / ? / ? | |
| 10.09.1944 | 25 / ? / ? | |
| 11.09.1944 | 25 / ? / ? | |
| 12.09.1944 | 20 / ? / ? | |
| 13.09.1944 | 14 / ? / ? | |
| 14.09.1944 | 14 / ? / ? | |
| 15.09.1944 | 15 / ? / ? | |
| 16.09.1944 | 12 / ? / ? | |
| 17.09.1944 | 12 / ? / ? | |

| Date | Status | Remarks |
|---|---|---|
| 18.09.1944 | 15 / ? / ? | |
| 19.09.1944 | 13 / ? / ? | |
| 20.09.1944 | 17 / ? / ? | |
| 21.09.1944 | 15 / ? / ? | |
| 22.09.1944 | 17 / ? / ? | |
| 23.09.1944 | 15 / ? / ? | |
| 24.09.1944 | 17 / ? / ? | |
| 25.09.1944 | 17 / ? / ? | 16 Panthers reported later |
| 26.09.1944 | 17 / ? / ? | |
| 27.09.1944 | 21 / ? / ? | |
| 28.09.1944 | 21 / ? / ? | |
| 30.09.1944 | 22 / ? / ? | |
| 01.10.1944 | 22 / 8 / 6 | Included are four Befehlspanther as operational |
| 02.10.1944 | 22 / ? / ? | |
| 03.10.1944 | 22 / ? / ? | Another report states 26 Panthers operational |
| 04.10.1944 | 22 / ? / ? | |
| 05.10.1944 | 22 / ? / ? | |
| 06.10.1944 | 24 / ? / ? | |
| 07.10.1944 | 25 / ? / ? | |
| 08.10.1944 | 27 / ? / ? | 25 Panthers reported later |
| 09.10.1944 | 27 / ? / ? | Another report states 22 Panthers operational |
| 10.10.1944 | 19 / ? / ? | |
| 11.10.1944 | 10 / ? / ? | |
| 12.10.1944 | 12 / ? / ? | |
| 13.10.1944 | 11 / ? / ? | |

| Date | Status | Remarks |
|---|---|---|
| 14.10.1944 | 13 / ? / ? | |
| 15.10.1944 | 13 / ? / ? | |
| 16.10.1944 | 11 / ? / ? | |
| 17.10.1944 | 11 / ? / ? | |
| 18.10.1944 | 15 / ? / ? | |
| 19.10.1944 | 16 / ? / ? | |
| 20.10.1944 | 18 / ? / ? | |
| 21.10.1944 | 15 / ? / ? | |
| 22.10.1944 | 14 / ? / ? | Seven Panthers reported later |
| 23.10.1944 | 14 / ? / ? | Another report states 19 Panthers operational |
| 24.10.1944 | 17/ ? / ? | |
| 25.10.1944 | 16 / ? / ? | |
| 26.10.1944 | 17 / ? / ? | |
| 27.10.1944 | 15 / ? / ? | |
| 28.10.1944 | 15 / ? / ? | Eight Panthers reported later |
| 29.10.1944 | 15 / ? / ? | |
| 30.10.1944 | 15 / ? / ? | |
| 31.10.1944 | 15 / ? / ? | |
| 01.11.1944 | 15 / 12 / 2 | |
| 02.11.1944 | 14 / ? / ? | |
| 03.11.1944 | 14 / ? / ? | |
| 04.11.1944 | 14 / ? / ? | |
| 05.11.1944 | 15 / ? / ? | |
| 06.11.1944 | 17 / ? / ? | |
| 07.11.1944 | 15 / ? / ? | |

| Date | Status | Remarks |
|---|---|---|
| 08.11.1944 | 16 / ? / ? | |
| 09.11.1944 | 16 / ? / ? | |
| 10.11.1944 | 16 / ? / ? | |
| 11.11.1944 | 19 / ? / ? | |
| 12.11.1944 | 20 / ? / ? | Another report state 22 Panthers operational |
| 13.11.1944 | 20 / ? / ? | |
| 14.11.1944 | 20 / ? / ? | |
| 15.11.1944 | 20 / ? / ? | |
| 16.11.1944 | 20 / ? / ? | |
| 17.11.1944 | 20 / ? / ? | |
| 18.11.1944 | 22 / ? / ? | |
| 19.11.1944 | 21 / ? / ? | |
| 20.11.1944 | 22 / ? / ? | |
| 21.11.1944 | 23 / ? / ? | |
| 22.11.1944 | 22 / ? / ? | |
| 23.11.1944 | 22 / ? / ? | |
| 24.11.1944 | 21 / ? / ? | |
| 27.11.1944 | 9 / ? / ? | Another report says 22 Panthers operational |
| 01.12.1944 | 22 / 5 / 2 | |
| 02.12.1944 | 22 / ? / ? | |
| 03.12.1944 | 27 / ? / ? | |
| 04.12.1944 | 27 / ? / ? | |
| 05.12.1944 | 27 / ? / ? | |
| 06.12.1944 | 27 / ? / ? | |
| 07.12.1944 | 27 / ? / ? | |

| Date | Status | Remarks |
|---|---|---|
| 08.12.1944 | 27 / ? / ? | |
| 09.12.1944 | 27 / ? / ? | |
| 10.12.1944 | 27 / ? / ? | |
| 11.12.1944 | 27 / ? / ? | |
| 12.12.1944 | 27 / ? / ? | |
| 17.12.1944 | 21 / ? / ? | |
| 22.12.1944 | 21 / ? / ? | |
| 29.12.1944 | 27 / ? / ? | |
| 30.12.1944 | 21 / ? / ? | |
| 31.12.1944 | 27 / ? / ? | |
| 01.01.1945 | 20 / 7 / 2 | |
| 02.01.1945 | 24 / ? / ? | |
| 03.01.1945 | 6 / ? / ? | |
| 04.01.1945 | 10 / ? / ? | |
| 05.01.1945 | 10 / ? / ? | |
| 06.01.1945 | 10 / ? / ? | |
| 07.01.1945 | 10 / ? / ? | |
| 11.01.1945 | 9 / ? / ? | |
| 13.01.1945 | 12 / ? / ? | Eight Panthers also reported on the same day |
| 15.01.1945 | 7 / ? / ? | Included three Befehlspanther as operational, also five Bergepantherss are operational as well |
| 16.01.1945 | 9/ ? / ? | |
| 17.01.1945 | 4 / 4 / 2 | 14 Panthers still in rail transit |
| 18.01.1945 | 4 / ? / ? | 14 Panthers unloaded in Veszprém |
| 19.01.1945 | 10/ ? / ? | |
| 20.01.1945 | 1 / ? / ? | |

| Date | Status | Remarks |
|---|---|---|
| 21.01.1945 | 1 / ? / ? | Two Panthers reported later |
| 22.01.1945 | 3 / ? / ? | |
| 23.01.1945 | 5 / ? / ? | |
| 24.01.1945 | 1 / ? / ? | |
| 25.01.1945 | -/ ? / ? | Three Panthers later reported |
| 26.01.1945 | 1 / ? / ? | |
| 27.01.1945 | 3 / ? / ? | |
| 28.01.1945 | 3 / ? / ? | |
| 30.01.1945 | 3 / ? / ? | |
| 01.02.1945 | 3 / 11 / 3 | Three Bergepanthers are also operational, both Befehlspanthers are in repair |
| 02.02.1945 | 3 / ? / ? | |
| 03.02.1945 | - / ? / ? | |
| 04.02.1945 | 3 / ? / ? | |
| 05.02.1945 | 3 / ? / ? | |
| 06.02.1945 | 3 / ? / ? | Later four Panthers reported operational |
| 07.02.1945 | 3 / ? / ? | |
| 10.02.1945 | 7 / ? / ? | |
| 12.02.1945 | 2 / ? / ? | |
| 13.02.1945 | 10 / 5 / 1 | |
| 15.02.1945 | 11 / 3 / 2 | Included one Befehlspanther as being operational and four Bergepantherss operational as well |
| 17.02.1945 | 12 / ? / ? | |
| 18.02.1945 | 12 / ? / ? | |
| 19.02.1945 | 12 / 2 / 2 | |
| 20.02.1945 | 12 / ? / ? | |

| Date | Status | Remarks |
|---|---|---|
| 21.02.1945 | 12 / ? / ? | |
| 24.02.1945 | 9 / ? / ? | |
| 26.02.1945 | 9 / ? / ? | |
| 28.02.1945 | 9 / ? / ? | |
| 01.03.1945 | 9 / 5 / 2 | Included one Befehlspanther as operational and four Bergepantherss operational as well |
| 02.03.1945 | 9 / ? / ? | |
| 03.03.1945 | 9 / ? / ? | Another report from *Heeresgruppe Süd* states all 16 Panthers in working order |
| 04.03.1945 | 9 / 4 / 3 | |
| 05.03.1945 | 9 / 6 / 1 | |
| 06.03.1945 | 5 / ? / ? | |
| 10.03.1945 | 8 / ? / ? | |
| 11.03.1945 | 8 / 6 / 2 | |
| 12.03.1945 | 8 / ? / ? | |
| 13.03.1945 | 8 / ? / ? | |
| 14.03.1945 | 8 / ? / ? | |
| 15.03.1945 | 8 / 6 / ? | Included one Befehlspanther as operational, also three Bergepanthers are also operational |
| 16.03.1945 | 10 / ? / ? | 10 Panthers in and around Magyaralmás |
| 17.03.1945 | 6 / ? / ? | Later, before midday, three Panthers reported fighting in the streets along with two Tigers as Soviet infantry go house to house (during the morning hours) and three Bergepanthers |
| 18.03.1945 | 4 / ? / ? | Four Panthers and two Bergepanthers operational and one Bergepanthers under tow due to track damage |
| 19.03.1945 | 3 / ? / ? | counter attack from Guttamási |
| 20.03.1945 | 3 / ? / ? | |
| 21.03.1945 | 3 / ? / ? | |
| 24.03.1945 | - / ? / ? | |

| Date | Status | Remarks |
|---|---|---|
| 25.03.1945 | - / ? / ? | |
| 26.03.1945 | - / ? / ? | |
| 28.03.1945 | - / ? / ? | |
| 30.03.1945 | - / ? / ? | |
| 31.03.1945 | - / ? / ? | Two Bergepanthers reported operational |
| 01.04.1945 | - / 1 / 2 | two Bergepanthers on hand |
| 04.04.1945 | 2 / ? / ? | With SS-*Kampfgruppe* Kuhn, *III./SS-Panzergrenadier-Regiment 5 'Totenkopf'*, in the area of Gotzendorf and Pischelsdorf |
| 05.04.1945 | - / 3 / ? | Two Bergepanthers on hand |
| 06.04.1945 | 2 / ? / ? | |
| 09.04.1945 | 1 / ? / ? | In Vienna |
| 10.04.1945 | - / 1 / 2 | |
| 11.04.1945 | 1 / ? / ? | In the Prater District |
| 12.04.1945 | 1 / ? / ? | Also two Bergepanthers reported operational as well |
| 13.04.1945 | 1 / ? / ? | In the Prater district of Wien |
| 14.04.1945 | 1 / ? / ? | In the area of Stockerau |
| 15.04.1945 | 1 / 1 / ? | Also two Bergepanthers operational as well |
| 25.04.1945 | 2 / ? / ? | Two Bergepanthers in short term repair |
| 01.05.1945 | 2 / ? / ? | |
| 05.05.1945 | 2 / ? / ? | |
| 06.05.1945 | 2 / ? / ? | |
| 07.05.1945 | 2 / ? / ? | Also two Bergepanthers operational as well |
| 08.05.1945 | 2 / ? / ? | Also two Bergepanthers operational as well |

# APPENDIX 6

★ ★ ★

## Total Losses of *I./SS-Panzer-Regiment 3* 1944-1945

### 25 JULY 1944 (TWO PANTHERS LOST)

Two Panthers of *1. Kompanie* were knocked out by Soviet anti-tank gunfire, near the Siedlce-Mordy railway line, during an attack to free the Siedlce-Miedzyrec road, south-east of Siedlce. One Panther was commanded by *SS-Oberscharführer* Ober, the other by *SS-Untersturmführer* von Rennenkampf; both were *Zugführer*. Von Rennenkampf's crew managed to escape had but all suffered burns as the Panther burst into flame.

### 26 JULY 1944 (EIGHT PANTHERS LOST)

One Panther (from *1. Kompanie*) was destroyed by Soviet artillery fire at the east exit of Siedlce. The Panther rolled off the road. Another two Panthers (from *3. Kompanie*) were knocked out along the Siedlce-Mordy road. One Panther (from *2. Kompanie*) was knocked out by Soviet anti-tank gunfire near Borki. Four Panthers were knocked out in Chromna as follows:

A Panther was struck in the hull by a 75mm round, another 75mm round penetrated the engine compartment and the main gun was damaged by a further hit from a 75mm round.

A second Panther was hit once in the rear of the hull.

A third Panther was struck in the side of the hull from an 85mm round

A forth Panther was hit four times by 45mm rounds in the running gear and engine compartment.

### 28 JULY 1944 ( FIVE PANTHERS LOST)

SS-*Kampfgruppe Meierdrees* suffered five total losses near Pruszyn-Pierki after the Panthers drove over anti-tank mines. This was reported at 1715 hours. The Panthers were from the *1. Kompanie* and the *Stabskompanie* of the *I./SS-Panzer-Regiment 3*.

### 29 JULY 1944 (ONE PANTHERS LOST )

One Panther from *4. Kompanie* was knocked out by Soviet tank fire on the outskirts of Siedlce (Panther 424). The Panther was hit once in the side of the turret by an 85mm round and another 85mm round struck the front of the turret. A third 85mm round hit the front of the hull.

### 30 JULY 1944 (NINE PANTHERS LOST)

One Panther (from *3. Kompanie*) was destroyed by Soviet tank fire during the street fighting for Siedlce. The Panther was hit by two rounds which penetrated the hull and ignited the main ammunition, destroying the Panther. Another three rounds from 75mm ammunition struck the hull but no penetration was reported by the Soviet examination team.

A second Panther was disabled by three 122mm tank rounds. The crew had blown the Panther up. The 122mm rounds failed to penetrate the armour.

Two Panthers were captured intact on the eastern edge of the town in working order.

Two Panthers were knocked out during the afternoon during a counterattack against the 3rd Guards Cavalry Division at the western exit of Siedlce on the highway heading in the direction of Broskow, Warsaw.

One Panther was knocked out on the corner of Kazimierzowska and Starowiejska Street. One Panther was knocked out in the central area of Siedlce.

A dug-in Panther was struck and knocked out next to the Church of St. Joseph on Sokolowska Street.

### 11 AUGUST 1944 (TWO PANTHERS LOST)

Both Panthers (from *4. Kompanie*) were knocked out on the eastern edge of Brzczowica by concealed Soviet anti-tank gunfire positioned at the northern end of the village.

### 19 AUGUST 1944 (TWO PANTHERS LOST)

One Panther was knocked out by Soviet tank fire, near Krusze. The Panther was hit by a 122mm round to the side of the hull. An 85mm round penetrated the turret. Another five rounds hit the hull which caused the main ammunition to explode.

Another Panther was knocked out in Roszczep. This Panther was struck by 85mm rounds in the hull and sides.

On 20 August 1944, *Armeeoberkommando 9* reported the foregoing four Panthers from *SS-Totenkopf* as total losses.

## 23 AUGUST 1944 (ONE PANTHER LOST)

A Panther (from *4. Kompanie*) was struck by a direct hit from Soviet artillery fire in the village of Guzowattka during a Soviet artillery barrage.

## 27 AUGUST 1944 (ONE PANTHER LOST)

A Panther (from 1. *Kompanie*) caught fire after sustaining fuel-line damage during a road march from Radzymin to Serock. The Panther was burnt out.

## 30 AUGUST 1944 (ONE PANTHER LOST)

This Panther was destroyed by a direct hit from a Soviet artillery round in Radzymin.

## 2 SEPTEMBER 1944 (FIVE PANTHERS LOST)

While in support of a battle group from the Hungarian 1st Cavalry Division during the fighting for Nadma, two Panthers were knocked out by Soviet anti-tank gunfire.

A Panther in Struga, suffered fuel-line damage and blew up – the turret was blown clear of the hull.

Two other Panthers were knocked out near Brzozowa.

## 12 SEPTEMBER 1944 (TWO PANTHERS LOST)

One Panther was knocked out by Soviet anti-tank gunfire during the fighting for Hill 104. Another Panther was knocked out near Zabki.

## 14 SEPTEMBER 1944 (FIVE PANTHERS LOST)

Two Panthers were knocked out by Soviet anti-tank gunfire near Elsnerow.

One Panther was knocked out during the withdrawal from Hill 104 after coming under heavy Soviet artillery fire.

One Panther was knocked out by Soviet tank fire near Drewniza

One Panther was knocked out during a counterattack near Kobylka.

## 15 SEPTEMBER 1944 (TWO PANTHERS LOST)

Two Panthers from *1. Kompanie* broke down and were abandoned due to the combat situation. Later, the crews returned to blow up both Panthers – the wrecks were left near Lewicpol.

## 10 OCTOBER 1944 (ONE PANTHER LOST)

One Panther from *1. Kompanie* was destroyed by a direct hit from Soviet artillery fire east of Rosopole.

## 11 OCTOBER 1944 (FIVE PANTHERS LOST)

Three Panthers (one them from *1. Kompanie*) are knocked out during a counterattack from Jozefow towards Michalow-Grabina.

A fourth Panther was knocked out just north of Michalow-Grabina by a 76mm round which hit the engine compartment.

Another Panther was knocked out by a 76mm round to the rear of the hull.

Two further Panthers were seriously damaged and required long-term repair.

## 17 OCTOBER 1944 (ONE PANTHER LOST)

One Panther from *1. Kompanie* is struck by Soviet artillery fire near Jozefow. On 18 October 1944 a demolition team return to the Panther and blow it up.

## 2 JANUARY 1945 (ONE PANTHER LOST)

This Panther was knocked out halfway along the road to Bajót, Dózsa György utca, in Lábatlan. The Panther came from *3. Kompanie.*

## 3 JANUARY 1945 (ONE PANTHER LOST)

While leaving Bajna, a column of *SS-Totenkopf* tanks comes under Soviet air attack; one Panther was destroyed by a direct hit from a bomb (Panther 301) [It cannot be proven and this contradicts the sources – editor's note]

## 5 JANUARY 1945 (TWO PANTHERS LOST)

Both Panthers were knocked out by Soviet anti-tank fire north-west of Szomor; both quickly caught fire. These Panthers were hit multiple times in the hull, running gear and turret. One of them was Panther I03.

## 7 JANUARY 1945 (ONE PANTHER LOST)

The Panther was knocked out in the woods south of Szomor by an SU-100 self-propelled gun (382nd Guards Self Propelled Artillery Regiment of the 1st Guards Mechanized Corps). During the advance, nine other Panthers suffered heavy battle damage.

## 18 JANUARY 1945 (TWO PANTHERS LOST)

Two Panthers left Szabadbattyan along the eastern exit road and approached the bridge crossing the Malom Canal. The first Panther crossed the bridge and approached the next bridge spanning the Nádor Canal where it was knocked out by Soviet anti-tank gunfire from the 10th Separate Anti-Tank Artillery Brigade. The second Panther fell through the bridge which collapsed under the weight of the tank. This Panther was abandoned.

## 21 JANUARY 1945 (TWO BEFEHLSPANTHERS AND TWO PANTHERS LOST)

After advancing along the Agárd-Gárdony route, two Befehlspanthers and another two Panthers (one of which was from *1. Kompanie*) were knocked out by Soviet anti-tank gunfire in a ravine just outside Kápolnásnyék, on the western edge of the village. During the advance the Panthers received murderous flanking anti-tank gunfire from the south and south-east of their positions.

## 27 JANUARY 1945 (ONE BEFEHLSPANTHER LOST)

One Befehlspanther of the regimental *Stabskompanie* was knocked out in Baracska by a single 85mm round from Soviet tank fire to the left side of the turret which killed two of the crew. [Editor's note: this cannot be proven and contradicts the sources.]

## 5 FEBRUARY 1945 (ONE BEFEHLSPANTHER LOST)

Befehlspanther I01 (from the *Stabskompanie*) was written off after being damaged on 2 January 1945 in Dunaalmás (see entry for events for 2 January 1945).

## 16 MARCH 1945 (FOUR PANTHERS LOST)

All four Panthers were lost 1.5km south-east of Magyaralmás during a counterattack in the direction of Borbala Puszta.

Panther 431 (an Ausf. A) was knocked out by a single 45mm anti-tank round which penetrated the hull just above the left side track. The tank also has the name 'Inge' painted on the back of the turret.

Another Panther Ausf. A was abandoned after the left track became bogged down in thick mud.

One Panther Ausf. G (turret number 323) was abandoned on the south-east exit road from Magyaralmás after suffering technical damage.

Another Panther Ausf. G (turret number122) was abandoned in the same area after breaking down; during an attempted recovery one of the crew was killed.

## 17 MARCH 1945 (SEVEN PANTHERS AND THREE BERGEPANTHERS LOST)

Befehlspanther I02 was knocked out near the *Abteilung* command post which was located at the first house in Magyaralmás on the northern edge of the village.

Two Panthers were knocked out on the eastern edge of Magyaralmás by Soviet rocket fire.

Two more Panthers (one of them carrying turret number 212) were knocked out near Hill 173 by a platoon of 57mm guns assigned to the 296th Guards Rifle

Regiment. Both Panthers were burnt-out wrecks. Hill 173 was next to the road junction leading to Fehérvárcsurgó.

One Panther was destroyed by Soviet rocket fire near the eastern edge of Magyaralmás.

Another Panther was abandoned on Kossuth utca following technical malfunction.

Also two SPWs were destroyed in Magyaralmás by rocket fire.

Two Bergepanthers were abandoned in Magyaralmás and another in a field about 800 metres east of Magyaralmás while trying to tow the Tiger of *SS-Hauptsturmführer* Ther, *Chef* of *9. Kompanie.*

## 18 MARCH 1945 (ONE BERGEPANTHER LOST)

The Bergepanthers had earlier thrown a track during a recovery operation and had to be recovered itself by another Bergepanther which appears to have been abandoned.

## 19 MARCH 1945 (TWO PANTHERS LOST)

Both Panthers were found abandoned on the eastern edge of Isztimér. They were discovered by elements of the 346th Guards Rifle Regiment from the 104th Guards Rifle Division at 1830 hours (Moscow time).

## 12 APRIL 1945 (ONE PANTHER LOST)

This Panther was knocked out by Soviet tank fire near the Reichs Bridge in Vienna.

## 8 MAY 1945 (TWO PANTHERS LOST)

The two Panthers from *Kampfgruppe Neff* were assembled in Noehagen bei Krems and were disabled by the crews. One Panther was blown up after the crew put explosive charges and hand grenades inside the turret. The crew dismantled the tracks of the second Panther and let it roll down a hill into a muddy field. Both Panthers were scrapped by a local firm two years later. Between the years 1945 and 1947, these Panthers were used as a playground by the local children.

Children took the ammunition out of the Panther that had been rolled into the field and tried to burn it.

The two Bergepanthers were abandoned as follows: one Bergepanthers in Rehberg, north of Krems; the other in Stratzing, along with a *Zugkraftwagen* from the *Instandsetzungs-Zug* of *9. Kompanie* and a Sd.Kfz. 7/2 with a 3.7cm anti-aircraft gun.

Three Shermans with 2cm Flak *Vierling* guns from *Kampfgruppe Neff* were also destroyed on this day.

NACHRICHTENZUG
101 102
AUFKLÄRUNGSZUG
103 104 105
1./SS-PZ.RGT. 3
101 102
111 112 113 114 115
121 122 123 124 125
131 132 133 134 135
2./SS-PZ.RGT. 3
201 202
211 212 213 214 215
221 222 223 224 225
231 232 233 234 235
3./SS-PZ.RGT. 3
301 302
311 312 313 314 315
321 322 323 324 325
331 332 333 334 335
4./SS-PZ.RGT. 3
401 402
411 412 413 414 415
421 422 423 424 425
431 432 433 434 435

# LIST OF SOURCES

★ ★ ★

## German ArchIVal Material (Bundesarchiv-Militärarchiv, Germany)

- RH 8 Heereswaffenamt
- RH 8 1/1427
- RH 8 1/1136
- RH 8 1/815

- RH 14 Chef Heeresrüstung und Befehlshaber Ersatzheer

- RH 11 Waffengenerale im OKH

- RH 12/6 Inspektion der Panzertruppen

- RH 2 OKH/Gen.St.des Heeres
- RH 2/1465

**RH 10 Generalinspekteur der Panzertruppen**

- RH 10/20
- RH 10/22
- RH 10/23
- RH 10/25
- RH 10/26
- RH 10/60
- RH 10/61
- RH 10/62
- RH 10/63
- RH 10/64
- RH 10/69
- RH 10/70
- RH 10/71
- RH 10/72
- RH 10/89
- RH 10/90
- RH 10/103
- RH 10/109
- RH 10/118
- RH 10/314
- RH 10/349
- RH 10/350

**Heeresgruppe Mitte**

- RH 09-II/098
- RH 09-II/099

**Heeresgruppe Mitte**

- RH 19-II/198, Parts 1, 2, 3 and 4
- RH 19-II/199, Parts 1, 2, and 3
- RH 19-II/203
- RH 19-II/213
- RH 19-II/214
- RH 19-II/215
- RH 19-II/221
- RH 19-II/222
- RH 19-II/232
- RH 19-II/327

**Panzerarmeeoberkommando 1**

- RH 21-1/359
- RH 21-1/361
- RH 21-1/362
- RH 21-1/363
- RH 21-1/364
- RH 21-1/365
- RH 21-1/366
- RH 21-1/368
- RH 21-1/371

**Armeeoberkommando 2**

- RH 20-2/931
- RH 20-2/932
- RH 20-2/933
- RH 20-2/934
- RH 20-2/935
- RH 20-2/936
- RH 20-2/937
- RH 20-2/938
- RH 20-2/939
- RH 20-2/940
- RH 20-2/941
- RH 20-2/942
- RH 20-2/943
- RH 20-2/944
- RH 20-2/945
- RH 20-2/946
- RH 20-2/947
- RH 20-2/988
- RH 20-2/1582

**Armeeoberkommando 4**

- RH 20-4/560
- RH 20-4/561
- RH 20-4/562
- RH 20-4/563
- RH 20-4/564
- RH 20-4/570
- RH 20-4/571

**Armeeoberkommando 6**

- RH 20-6/507
- RH 20-6/830
- RH 20-6/831
- RH 20-6/833
- RH 20-6/836
- RH 20-6/837
- RH 20-6/907

**Armeeoberkommando 8**

- RH 20-8/223
- RH 20-8/225
- RH 20-8/226
- RH 20-8/227
- RH 20-8/230

**Armeeoberkommando 9**

- RH 20-9/595
- RH 20-9/230
- RH 20-9/231
- RH 20-9/233

**I. SS-Panzerkorps**

- I. SS-Panzerkorps, Anhang zu KTB Nr 5, 10 April 1943-28 May 1943

**II. SS-Panzerkorps**

- RS 2-2/3
- RS 4/1460

- RH 2-Karte Lage Ost 1944-1945
- RH 2-2746, 24 July 1944
- RH 2-2747, 25 July 1944
- RH 2-2748, 26 July 1944
- RH 2-2749, 27 July 1944
- RH 2-2750, 28 July 1944
- RH 2-2751, 29 July 1944
- RH 2-2752, 30 July 1944
- RH 2-2753, 31 July 1944

- RH 2-2754, 1 August 1944
- RH 2-2755, 2 August 1944
- RH 2-2771, 18 August 1944
- RH 2-2785, 1 September 1944
- RH 2-2787, 3 September 1944
- RH 2-2805, 21 September 1944
- RH 2-2807, 23 September 1944
- RH 2-2815, 1 October 1944
- RH 2-2820, 6 October 1944
- RH 2-2823, 9 October 1944
- RH 2-2837, 23 October 1944
- RH 2-2846, 1 November 1944
- RH 2-2853, 8 November 1944
- RH 2-2870, 25 November 1944
- RH 2-2872, 27 November 1944
- RH 2-2876, 1 December 1944
- RH 2-2877, 2 December 1944
- RH 2-2878, 3 December 1944
- RH 2-2879, 4 December 1944
- RH 2-2880, 5 December 1944
- RH 2-2881, 6 December 1944
- RH 2-2882, 7 December 1944
- RH 2-2883, 8 December 1944
- RH 2-2884, 9 December 1944
- RH 2-2886, 11 December 1944
- RH 2-2902, 20 December 1944
- RH 2-2904, 21 December 1944
- RH 2-2907, 23 December 1944
- RH 2-5263, 5 January 1945
- RH 2-5257, 11 January 1945
- RH 2-5280, 13 January 1945
- RH 2-5298, 20 January 1945
- RH 2-5316, 25 January 1945
- RH 2-5336, 31 January 1945
- RH 2-5339, 1 February 1945
- RH 2-5349, 3 February 1945
- RH 2-5355, 5 February 1945
- RH 2-5367, 8 February 1945
- RH 2-5385, 13 February 1945
- RH 2-5312, 15 February 1945
- RH 2-5391, 15 February 1945
- RH 2-5403, 18 February 1945
- RH 2-5408, 20 February 1945
- RH 2-5421, 24 February 1945
- RH 2-5423, 25 February 1945
- RH 2-5433, 1 March 1945
- RH 2-5435, 2 March 1945
- RH 2-5448, 8 March 1945
- RH 2-5455, 11 March 1945
- RH 2-5457, 12 March 1945
- RH 2-5473, 17 March 1945
- RH 2-5486, 22 March 1945
- RH 2-5491, 24 March 1945
- RH 2-5519, 25 March 1945
- RH 2-5508, 30 March 1945
- RH 2-5512, 1 April 1945
- RH 2-6909, 17 April 1945

- *SS-FHA*.Abt org 1942/43 and OKH.Abt.org 1942
- NS 19-2569
- NS 33/232
- NS 33/233

- SS-T Vermissten-Bildliste DRK

**Nachlass Vopersal**

- N756 133b SS-Panzer-Regiment 3
- N756 134a SS-Stug.Abt. 3

## NARA Microfilm (USA)

**Armeeoberkommando 4**

- T312-239
- T312-243

- T312-246
- T312-247

**Armeeoberkommando 2**
- T312-1316
- T312-1317
- T312-1318
- T312-1319
- T312-1324

**Armeeoberkommando 8**
- T312-64
- T312-65
- T312-67
- T312-68
- T312-69
- T312-70

**Armeeoberkommando 9**
- T312-339
- T312-343
- T312-344
- T312-345
- T312-347
- T312-348

**Heeresgruppe Mitte**
- T311-216
- T311-217
- T311-218
- T311-227
- T311-228
- T312-233

**OB West**
- T311-28 Transport movements for *I./SS-Panzer-Regiment 3* (Panther)

**Heeresgruppe Süd**
- T311-160
- T311-161
- T311-162
- T311-163

**II. SS-Pz.Korps**
- T354-605
- T354-606
- T354-608
- T354-118
- T354-119
- T354-120

**Other**
- T314-1495 LVII. Panzerkorps QM
- T314-658 XX. Armeekorps
- T314-659 XX. Armeekorps
- T314-397 VIII. Armeekorps
- T78-418 Gen.St.d.H/Org Abt
- T78-525
- T78-719 Waffen-SS
- T733-7 Waffen-SS guide roll.
- T78-718 Panzer-Division and Panther-Abt.
- T78-622
- T78-623
- T78-624
- T78-619
- T77-1422
- T175-108

**Imperial War Museum (United Kingdom)**
- MI 14/140 OKW+OKH Strengths and Casualty figures, Stand 15 April 1945
- MI 14/145 Section F, 12 April 1945

- MI 14/270 22 June April 1 TO 31 March 1945
- MI 14/371.
- AL 2517 Strength of Waffen-SS Feb-April 1945
- MI14/515 Band II Waffen-SS units 6 June 1944
- AL 2542 Generalinspekteur der Panzertruppen, Feb/April 1945
- MI 14/150 Section B-Panzarlage Ost Mai/Juni 1944
- MI 14/260 ErsatzHeer
- MI 14/124 Section A-C, 2 April 1945 to 18 April 1945, 31 March 1945 to 25 April 1945

**Central Archives of Ministry of Defence (Russia)**

- Reports of Russian units who engaged *3. SS-Panzer-Division 'Totenkopf'* (March 1944 to March 1945) and *IV. SS-Panzerkorps*

- 79th Rifle Corps
- 49th Guards Rifle Corps
- 26th Guards Rifle Corps
- 25th Guards Rifle Division
- 94th Guards Rifle Division
- 110th Guards Rifle Division
- 1st Guards Airborne Division
- 9th Guards Army
- 6th Guards Army
- 6th Guards Tank Army
- 1st Guards Mechanized Corps
- 9th Guards Mechanized Corps
- 5th Guards Tank Corps
- 5th Guards Cavalry Corps
- 37th Guards Rifle Corps
- 38th Guards Rifle Corps
- 39th Guards Rifle Corps
- 18th Tank Corps
- 23rd Tank Corps
- 100th Guards Rifle Division
- 103th Guards Rifle Division
- 104th Guards Rifle Division
- 105th Guards Rifle Division
- 107th Guards Rifle Division
- 113th Rifle Division
- 114th Guards Rifle Division
- 98th Guards Rifle Division
- 99th Guards Rifle Division
- 252nd Rifle Division
- 63rd Cavalry Division
- 12th Cavalry Division
- 220th Cavalry Regiment
- 47th Cavalry Regiment
- 1st Guards Mechanized Brigade
- 2nd Guards Mechanized Brigade
- 3rd Guards Mechanized Brigade
- 54th Guards Artillery Brigade
- 90th Guards Cannon Brigade
- 170th Tank Brigade
- 20th Tank Brigade
- 22nd Tank Brigade
- 46th Guards Tank Brigade
- 18th Guards Mechanized Brigade
- 30th Guards Mechanized Brigade
- 31st Guards Mechanized Brigade
- 18th Guards Tank Regiment
- 33rd Guards Tank Regiment
- 83rd Guards Tank Regiment
- 85th Guards Tank Regiment
- 62nd Guards Heavy Tank Regiment
- 484th Anti-Tank Artillery Regiment
- 1,438th Self-Propelled Artillery Regiment
- 382nd Self-Propelled Artillery Regiment

- $49^{th}$ Artillery Anti-Tank Brigade
- $1,008^{th}$ Artillery Anti-Tank Regiment
- $1,249^{th}$ Artillery Anti-Tank Regiment
- $10^{th}$ Artillery Anti-Tank Brigade
- $9^{th}$ Guards Tank Brigade
- $74^{th}$ Guards Anti-Tank Artillery Regiment
- $300^{th}$ Guards Rifle Regiment
- $302^{nd}$ Guards Rifle Regiment
- $303^{rd}$ Guards Rifle Regiment
- $317^{th}$ Guards Rifle Regiment
- $322^{nd}$ Guards Rifle Regiment
- $324^{th}$ Guards Rifle Regiment
- $328^{th}$ Guards Rifle Regiment
- $332^{nd}$ Guards Rifle Regiment
- $296^{th}$ Guards Rifle Regiment
- $297^{th}$ Guards Rifle Regiment
- $299^{th}$ Guards Rifle Regiment
- $346^{th}$ Guards Rifle Regiment
- $172^{nd}$ Guards Mortar Regiment
- $106^{th}$ Guards Anti-Tank Artillery Battalion
- $3^{rd}$ Guards Motorised Rifle Battalion
- $17^{th}$ Air Army
- $10^{th}$ Assault Air Corps
- $47^{th}$ Army
- $2^{nd}$ Guards Cavalry Corps
- $11^{th}$ Tank Corps
- $77^{th}$ Rifle Corps
- $125^{th}$ Rifle Corps
- $129^{th}$ Rifle Corps
- $60^{th}$ Rifle Division
- $306^{th}$ Air Assault Division
- $912^{th}$ Self-Propelled Artillery Regiment
- $1513^{th}$ Self Propelled Artillery Regiment
- $1523^{rd}$ Self Propelled Artillery Regiment

# BIBLIOGRAPHY

★ ★ ★


- Bacyk, Norbert: *Warsaw 2: The Battle for Praga: July - September 1944* (Operations: East Front 1944) (v. 2). Leandoer and Ekholm, 2009.
- Brettner, Friedrich: *Die letzten Kämpfe des II. Weltkrieges vom Neusiedler See zur Donau, March und Thaya: 2. SS Panzerkorps - 8. Deutsche Armee.* Eigenverlag, 2004.
- Cerff, Karl: *Die Waffen-SS im Wehrmachtbericht.* Munin Verlag, Osnabrück, 1971.
- Comrades Association: *Die IV. (schw.)/SS-Art.Rgt. 3.* 1985
- Comrades Association: *Im gleichen Schritt und Tritt. Dokumentation der 16. SS-Panzergrenadieerdivision "Reichsführer-SS".* Schild Verlag, 1998.
- Fuchs, Fritz: *Statt Abitur zur Waffen-SS.* 2014.
- Glantz, David M.: *Red Storm over the Balkans.* University Press of Kansas, 2006.
- Hinze, Rolf: *East Front Drama 1944.* J. J. Fedorowicz Publishing, 1997.
- Jentz, Thomas: *Panzertruppen 2. The Complete Guide to the Creation & Combat Employment of Germany's Tank Force, 1943-1945. Formations, Organizations, Tactics Combat Reports, Unit Strengths, Statistics.* Schiffer Publishing, 1996.
- Kapowka, Edward: *Battle for Siedlce,* July 1944.
- Krätschmer, Ernst-Günther: *Die Ritterkreuzträger der Waffen-SS.* Preussisch Oldendorf, Schütz Verlag, 1982.
- Maier, Georg: *Drama between Budapest and Vienna.* J. J. Fedorowicz Publishing, 2004.
- Neuman, Joachim: *Die 4. Panzer-Division 1943-1945. Bericht und Betrachtung zu den letzten zwei Kriegsjahren im Osten.* Selbstverlag, Bonn, 1989.
- Niepold, Gerd: *Battle for White Russia: The Destruction of Army Group Centre, June 1944.* Brassey's, 1987.
- Nipe, George M. Jr.: *Decision in the Ukraine, Summer 1943: II. SS and III. Panzerkorps.* J. J. Fedorowicz Publishing, 1996.

- Nipe, George M. Jr.: *Last Victory in Russia: The SS-Panzerkorps and Manstein's Kharkov Counteroffensive, February-March 1943*. Schiffer Publishing, 2000.
- Oosterling, Paul and Fischer, Hans and Erlings, Ron: *SS-Standartenführer Johannes Mühlenkamp – Kommandeur des SS-Panzerregiment 5 „Wiking" und seine Männer.* Band I und II. De Krijger, 2005.
- Syndor, Charles W. Jr.: *Soldiers of Destruction*. Princeton University Press, 1990.
- Tieke, Wilhelm and Rebstock, Friedrich: *Im letzten Aufgebot. Die 18. SS-Freiwilligen-Panzergrenadier-Division HORST WESSEL*. Band I und II. Nation Europa Verlag, 2000.
- Tieke, Wilhelm: *SS-Panzer-Brigade Westfalen, March-April 1945*. J. J. Fedorowicz Publishing, 2003.
- Trang, Charles: *Totenkopf.* Editions Heimdal, 2008.
- Trang, Charles: *Totenkopf Archive*. Casemate Pub & Book Dist Llc, 2011.
- Ungváry, Krisztián: *Battle for Budapest*. I B Tauris, 2011.
- Volkner, Werner: *Many Rivers I have Crossed*. 2004.
- Vopersal, Wolfgang: *Soldaten, Kämpfer, Kameraden*. Marsch und Kämpfe der SS-*Totenkopf-Division.* Band IIIa, Band IIIb, Band *IVa*, Band IVb, Band Va and Band Vb. Osnabrück, 1987-1991.
- Ullrich, Karl: *Like a Cliff in the Ocean. A History of the 3. SS-Panzer-Division "Totenkopf"*. J. J. Fedorowicz Publishing, 2002.
- Yerger, Mark C.: *Waffen-SS Commanders: The Army, Corps and Divisional Leaders of a Legend: Augsberger to Kreutz* (vol. 1). Schiffer Publishing, 1997.
- Yerger, Mark C.: *Waffen-SS Commanders: The Army, Corps and Divisional Leaders of a Legend: Krüger to Zimmermann* (vol. 2). Schiffer Publishing, 1999.
- Weidemann, Gerd-Axel: *Unser Regiment : Reiter-Regiment 2 - Panzer-Regiment 24*. Gross-Umstad, Ernst J. Dohany, 1983.
- Zährl, Hugo: *Vier Jahre in vorderster Front.* Munin-Verlag, 2007.
- Zetterling, Niklas and Frankson, Anders: *Kursk 1943*. Routledge, 2000.
- Wydawnictwo Militaria 243: *Wien 1945*.
- Wydawnictwo Militaria 246: *Budapest-Balaton 1945*.
- Militaria Nr 1(5) XX Wieku Nr 226165, *Tigers of the 3 SS-Panzer-Division 'Totenkopf' in Poland 1944,* C/O of Robert Wrobwelski.
- Militaria Magazine: *Tank Battle of Siedlce, July 1944.*

**Manuscripts**

- *Chronik der I./SS-Panzer-Regiment 3* (fragments only).
- Comrades Association: *1. and 2. Kompanie/SS-Pz.-Rgt. 3.*
- *Pionierchronik Pioniereinheiten der 3. SS-Panzer-Division 'Totenkopf.'*

## Interviews

- Report of Fritz Edelmann, *II./SS-Panzer-Regiment 3*
- *With SS-Panzer-Regiment 3 1943-1945*, report by former *SS-Oberscharführer* Horst Marx, *5. Kompanie/SS-Panzer-Regiment 3*
- Report of Kurt Söhrmann, *I./SS-Panzer-Regiment 3 1944 to 1945*
- Report of Hans Fenn, *I./SS-Panzer-Regiment 3 1945*
- Report of Franz Gschwandtner *I./SS-Panzer-Regiment 3 1945, Berge-Zug*
- Report of Gunter Trappe, *SS-Panzer-Regiment 3*
- Report of Rolf Stettner, *SS-Panzer-Regiment 3*
- Report of Heinz Zimmer, *SS-Panzer-Regiment 3*
- Report of Georg Fredrich Naumann, *SS-Panzer-Regiment 3*
- Report of Georg Fredrich Edelmann, *SS-Panzer-Regiment 3*
- Report of Norbert Hartmann, *SS-Panzer-Regiment 3*
- Report of Ernst Mertens, *7. Kompanie/SS-Panzer-Regiment 3*
- Interviews with veterans from *SS-Panzer-Regiment 3* conducted between 15 May 2011 and 18 May 2011

## Internet

- Missing Lynx Forums, Axis forces, post by David Bryden 22 March 2010 dealing with Panzer wrecks found at the Vienna Arsenal.
- Email via Oliver van Hettinga/Hans Fenn of *I./SS-Panzer-Regiment 3* discussing the Abteilung's activities in Hungary during 1945.
- Emails between myself and Ernest Chris Bacher regarding the wartime situation in Guttamási and Isztimér, during March 1945.
- Letter from Wolfgang Vopersal to Dr Manfried Rauchensteiner, *Einsatz der 3 SS-Pz Div 'Totenkopf', Endkampf in Österreich, 11th July 1969*, and sent via email.

## Field Trip to Hungary 10 September 2011-19 September 2011

- Site visits
- Magyaralmás
- Sőréd
- Bodajk
- Mór

**Thanks to the following people for their help and advice:**

- Jeff Dugdale
- John P. Moore
- Mirko Bayerl
- Kamen Nevenkin
- Dietrich Wolf
- Martin Block
- Oilver van Hettinga
- Max Reisner
- Dr. Martin Riegal (C/O of Oliver van Hettinga)
- Werner Volkner, *4. Bttr./SS-Flak Abteilung* 3
- Kurt Söhrmann, *Stabskompanie I./SS-Panzer-Regiment 3*
- Hans Fenn, *3. Kompanie I./SS-Panzer-Regiment 3*
- Franz Gschwandtner, *Panzer-Werkstattzug I./SS-Panzer-Regiment 3*
- Niklas Zetterling
- Robert Wrobwelski, Militaria XX Wieku Publishing
- Piet Duits
- Charles Trang
- Sebastian Remus
- Hans Weber
- Simon Vosters
- Timm Hassler
- Wojciech Grzegorz Stanczyk
- Adam Havasi and Andres Hege from the Hungarian Battlefield Archaeological Society
- Jan Hendrick
- Special mention to Didier Lodeau and Fred Deprun for their help regarding Mailly-le-Camp

# PHOTOS

Portrait of *SS-Sturmann* Kurt Söhrmann, the radio operator in *SS-Sturmbannführer* Meierdrees' Befehlspanther. (C/O Hr Sohrmann)

Befehlspanther I01 under cover against possible air attack. The picture was taken in Nowo Miastro in Poland during December 1944. (C/O Hr Sohrmann)

*SS-Unterscharführer* Kurt Söhrmann standing next to Befehlspanther I01, Nowo Miastro, December 1944. (C/O Hr Sohrmann)

Befehlspanther I01 is in the background; standing in front is
*SS-Unterscharführer* Georg Kasehage and Sepp Hirsch. (C/O Hr Sohrmann)

Standing from left to right in front of Befehlspanther I01 are *SS-Oberscharführer* Beetsch from the *Instandsetzungs-Staffel* of *Stabskompanie*, *SS-Unterscharführer* Hirsch (driver) and *SS-Oberscharführer* Ernst Horch, also from the *Instandsetzungs-Staffel* of the *Stabskompanie.* (C/O Hr Sohrmann)

The same three men, Beetsch, Hirsch and Horch standing in front of Meierdrees' Panther. (C/O Hr Sohrmann)

Befehlspanther I01 and I02 loaded on rail transport ready for departure to Hungary from Nasielsk, near Modlin on 26 December 1944. (C/O Hr Sohrmann)

A post war photograph showing a wedding party in Lábatlan.
The Panther Ausf. A was knocked out on 2 January 1945 along Dózsa György utca during *Operation 'Konrad'*. The Panther formally belonged to *3. Kompanie.* (via the Internet)

A Befehlspanther from *Stabskompanie* of *SS-Panzer-Regiment 3*. The Panther was hit on the left side of the turret by an 85mm round which killed two of the crew on 27 January 1945 near Baracska. The Panther was later towed to a collection point in Baracska. The trophy number Nr. 87 was later changed to Nr 132 in March 1945. (TsAMO)

The first recruits gather at the Panzer-Kaserne, Weimar-Buchenwald, during June 1942 for *SS-Panzer-Abteilung 4(III)* (Author's collection)

On 30 November 1942, *SS-Panzer-Abteilung 4(III)* took delivery of a number of Panzer IIIs and Panzer IVs in Angouleme, France. (Author's collection)

Photograph of the same delivery of Panzers from 30 November 1942 in Angouleme. Some of the Panzer IIIs were issued to *2. Kompanie* and the *Panzer-Aufklärungszug* in the regimental *Stabskompanie.* (Author's collection)

The *1. Kompanie* of *I./SS-Panzer-Regiment 3* on parade in a French barracks during Case Anton, the occupation of Vichy France. This photo was taken during December 1942.

The *1. Kompanie* of *I./SS-Panzer-Regiment 3* form up for an inspection by Spanish Army officers in Rivesaltes. (Authors collection)

Panzer crews of *4. (schwere) Kompanie*, along with a Panzer III in the background. Taken at Fallingbostel on 2 January 1943. The Kompanie Panzer IIIs were delivered 1 January 1943. (Author's collection)

Panzer IIIs and Tiger Is of *4. (schwere) Kompanie* in Poltava on 21 February 1943. (Author's collection)

All these Panthers were knocked out in September 1944 and towed to a collection point in Pultusk for scrapping. The photograph was taken on 11 October 1944 by a War Correspondent from the 1st Belorussian Front (C/O TsAMO)

Elements of *SS-Panzer-Regiment 3* entered Szomor on 5 January 1945 during *Operation 'Konrad'*. The Panzer IVs and the Sturmgeschütz IIIs belong to *6.* and *8. Kompanie.* The Panther in the background is from *3. Kompanie.* (C/O Mirko Bayerl)

*SS-Hauptsturmführer* Meierdrees photographed along with two other officers from *I./SS-Panzer-Regiment 3* in the Soviet Union during May 1943. (C/O Reif)

*SS-Hauptsturmführer* Meierdrees photographed with
the same two officers. Note that Meierdrees and the *Untersturmführer* standing
next to him seem to be wearing army issue Panzer jackets. (C/O Reif)

Portrait of *SS-Obersturmführer* Reifkogel wearing the Knight's Cross. (C/O Reif)

With his back turned *SS-Sturmbannführer* is Bochmann, commanding officer of *SS-Panzer-Regiment* 3, as he addresses men of *1. Kompanie* after awarding *SS-Obersturmführer* Reifkogel with the Knight's Cross during August 1943. (C/O Reif)

*Befehlspanther* I01 undergoing final checks before the start of *Operation 'Konrad'*. The photograph was taken on 1 January 1945 in Komárom. (C/O Hr Sohrmann)

*SS-Hauptscharführer* Dieter Baumann, standing in the centre, on a rail transport in Nasielsk on 26 December 1944. Dieter Baumann finally served as the *Panther-Abteilung*'s last *Adjutant* with the rank of *SS-Standartenoberjunker.* (C/O Hr Sohrmann)

*SS-Hauptscharführer* Baumann (sitting) next to the radio operator's hatch on his Panther Ausf. A tank on 26 December 1944. (C/O Hr Sohrmann)

*SS-Unterscharführer* Kurt Arp standing next to Befehlspanther I01 in Nowo Miastro, December 1944. Kurt Arp was the senior radio/signals technician for *I./SS-Panzer-Regiment 3.* (C/O Hr Sohrmann)

Standing in the centre dressed a motorcycle overcoat is the *Stabskompanie Schirrmeister*, Georg Kagel, inspecting the right side drive sprocket and track. Standing next to him is *SS-Unterscharführer* Kurt Söhrmann, Poland December 1944. (C/O Hr Sohrmann)

Befehlspanther I02; this Panther was the mount of the *Panther-Abteilung Adjutant*, *SS-Obersturmführer* Strobl. This photgraph was taken in early January 1945. (C/O Hr Sohrmann)

*SS-Unterscharführer* Kurt Söhrmann standing next to Befehlspanther I01 in Nowo Miastro, Poland December 1944. (C/O Hr Sohrmann)

Another photograph of Ernst Kirsch but this time taken a year later, in late 1944. Ernst Kirsch by this time had been promoted to *SS-Oberscharführer.* (C/O Hr Sohrmann)

Portrait of *SS-Unterscharführer* Ernst Kirsch who served with the *Stabskompanie* of *I./SS-Panzer-Regiment 3*. The photograph was taken in January 1943. (C/O Hr Sohrmann)